MICROCOMPUTER ART

Prentice-Hall, Inc., *Englewood Cliffs, New Jersey*
Prentice-Hall of Australia Pty Ltd, *Sydney*
Prentice-Hall Canada, Inc., *Toronto*
Prentice-Hall Hispanoamericana, S.A., *Mexico*
Prentice-Hall of India Private Ltd, *New Delhi*
Prentice-Hall International, Inc., *London*
Prentice-Hall of Japan, Inc., *Tokyo*
Prentice-Hall of Southeast Asia Pte Ltd, *Singapore*
Editora Prentice-Hall do Brasil Ltda, *Rio de Janeiro*
Whitehall Books Limited, *Wellington*

MICROCOMPUTER ART

ROSS EDWARDS

PRENTICE-HALL OF AUSTRALIA PTY LTD

Typeset by Computype Export,
Wellington, New Zealand.

Printed and bound in Australia by
Macarthur Press Sales Pty Ltd, Parramatta, N.S.W.

Cover design by Philip Eldridge.

1 2 3 4 5 89 88 87 86 85

ISBN 0 7248 0795 0
U.S. ISBN 0-13-580218-0

National Library of Australia
Cataloguing-in-Publication Data

Edwards, Ross, 1947-
    Microcomputer art.

    Bibliography.
    ISBN 0 7248 0795 0.

    1. Computer graphics. 2. Geometrical drawing — Computer
    programs. I. Title.

001. 64'43

CONTENTS

PREFACE

This book shows how to simulate the motion of a "Geometric Pen" or "Geometric Lathe" on the computer screen. These instruments were used in the nineteenth century to engrave geometric patterns on wood, metal, and even glass.

The patterns illustrated are drawn from a number of books published in the period 1851 to 1884, on the operation of the Geometric Lathe. The patterns are generated by programs (written in BASIC) which are rarely more than half a dozen lines long. Most patterns can be generated by the alteration of only one program line, by reference to the tables at the back of the book.

The book is written for general application with any small personal computer. It is not written specifically for any particular type of computer. The information at the end of Chapter 3 should assist you to convert the three or four program commands to suit most popular computers. However, the fact that so few BASIC commands are required to generate any pattern means that you will have little difficulty converting the hypothetical commands to any microcomputer. You need merely refer to the high-resolution graphics section of your user manual.

With the directions given in this book, not only will you be able to copy any illustrated pattern, but you can also experiment with your own patterns. The variety of patterns that can be produced is infinite.

This book is unique in combining two of the most ingenious of nineteenth and twentieth century technologies: nineteenth century geometric engraving and twentieth century computer graphics. It is hoped that this will give you a new direction in which to apply the remarkable graphic capabilities of your personal computer.

ROSS EDWARDS

1 Introduction

This book may well be the only work written on computers whose bibliography cites no reference less than 100 years old. Indeed, the earliest reference was published in 1752 and the main references were published in the period between 1851 and 1884.

This may seem paradoxical when the computer was not invented until around 1950. But in order to take a step forward in the field of Computer Art, it is necessary to look back in time.

THE GEOMETRIC LATHE

During the nineteenth century a number of books were published in England on the subject of ornamental engraving. These books record the intricate designs and patterns engraved by the Victorians on wood, metal, ivory, and glass.

Engraving was a fashionable recreation in the nineteenth century, although the expense no doubt limited its popularity. The cost of a lathe with a complete set of geometric attachments for ornamental engraving was £1500 in 1838. At that time a skilled mechanic was paid less than 8 cents an hour, so that such a lathe would cost over $200,000 in today's terms.

Nevertheless, the factory of the Holtzapffel family located at 64 Charing Cross Road, London, produced 2554 lathes between 1780 and 1914; almost twenty per year. Manufacture ceased at the end of the Victorian Era, when improved technology gave rise to other new and exciting recreations for the rich and eccentric.

This book shows how the beautiful designs engraved by the the ornamental lathe with its geometric attachment (which we will call the "Geometric Lathe") can now be reproduced on the computer screen. No knowledge of mathematics is presumed and only an elementary knowledge of computer programming. Indeed, the programs necessary to plot these patterns are rarely more than half a dozen lines long.

In 1872 T.S. Bazley wrote of the Geometric Lathe:

> It is hardly possible to put it in motion, whatever be its adjustments, without obtaining a figure of symmetry and pleasing appearance.

Yet the beauty of such figures is not only in seeing the completed pattern as in watching the computer plot it progressively before one's eyes. This experience would have been denied the Victorians, as the cutting mechanism of the lathe would have partially obscured their vision.

THE PERSONAL COMPUTER

The instrument used for ornamental engraving in the nineteenth century had various physical limitations. The personal computer today has few. It is therefore possible to plot a wide variety of patterns not hitherto possible by mechanical means. Moreover, most patterns can be plotted by the computer in a matter of minutes.

The purpose of this book is twofold. First, to outline the principles involved in simulating the motion of the Geometric Lathe on the computer screen. Second, to provide a short index of patterns thus produced. Bazley wrote:

> The combinations of which the [Geometric Lathe] is susceptible are so varied and numerous that without some knowledge of the results to be expected from each of the several adjustments, much time may be lost in vague trials, and some desired effect be still unattained.

The subject of computer art is in its infancy. All that is required to get started is a small personal computer and a creative mind! Michelangelo once said: "A man paints with his brains and not with his hands." Ironically, his comments are even more appropriate with computer art than with traditional art.

Experimenting with new patterns requires amending or rewriting programs. This educational aspect of the book may be helpful to teachers, students, and others interested in computer literacy. The following verse, written over one hundred years ago, by H. Perigal seems curiously appropriate to the Geometric Lathe:

Experiment should be our guide.
Let, when we differ, none decide;
But each exert his zeal and sense,
In search of further evidence,
Till overwhelming facts bring out
The truth, so plain that none can doubt.
Where pride and prejudice abound
The truth is never to be found.

In 1873 H.S. Savory wrote of the Geometric Lathe (by coincidence the comment is equally applicable to the computer today):

It is the most fascinating instrument of ornamental turning; there is hardly a curve it is incapable of producing. It has all the elements of fascination; for it is, as far as any human powers can judge, infinite in the variety of forms that it can produce; and beautiful as the Author flatters himself are the specimens in this book, there are contained within the powers of the lathe, forms far more beautiful than any of them, which only require the ingenuity and taste of the operator to elicit.

The Victorian Era was a time when buildings, furniture, and the like were all adorned with motifs of Greek, Roman, Gothic, and other historical styles. Engraving was an expression of this preoccupation with ornamentation. In fact the Victorians engraved everything from eggshells to gold bullets used in Indian tiger-hunts! In generating the patterns in this book on your computer screen, you may well perceive the same Victorian exuberance.

2 The Geometric Pen

The predecessor of the Geometric Lathe was the "Geometric Pen." Invention of the pen is generally attributed to an Italian, Count Giovanni Battiste Suardi, who published a description of it in a book entitled *Nuovi Instrumento per la Desrizione di diverse Curve Antichi e Moderne* in 1752. The 12 change-wheels provided with this pen made it possible to produce 1273 different designs.

Inspiration for the Geometric Pen is discussed in Chapter 4. However, to put its invention in perspective, it should be mentioned that the Renaissance saw a proliferation of scientific instruments, including the quadrant, sextant, magnetic compass, microscope, telescope, and clock. More specifically it saw a proliferation of mathematical drawing instruments, including the compass (for drawing circles), cyclograph (for drawing arcs of large radiuses), pantagraph (for drawing enlargements and reductions), helicograph (for drawing spirals), elliptograph, parabolagraph, and of course, the Geometric Pen.

Description of the pen was first contained in an English publication by G. Adams, *Geometrical and Graphical Essays,* in 1791. Adams was a noted manufacturer of scientific instruments and made and sold a modified version of the pen. References to the Geometric Pen subsequently appeared in the English *Mechanics* magazine in 1829 and afterwards.

Figure 1 is taken from the *Penny Cyclopaedia* (1843), published under the aegis of the Society for the Diffusion of Useful Knowledge.

Accompanying the illustration was the following description:

This is an instrument invented by Suardi, an Italian, for drawing geometric curves. These curves may by combination be made to form an almost infinite variety of patterns. It is supported by three legs, bowed so as to allow room for the instrument

4

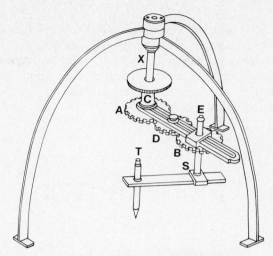

FIGURE 1   THE GEOMETRIC PEN

to work within them. These legs shut together by the joint at the top for the convenience of package. Attached to the joint is a stem or axis X, upon the lower end of which is fixed the toothed wheel A. This stem with its wheel, is stationery and all the other parts of the instruments move round it.

The pen itself traces a curve dependent upon the compound motion of the wheels, one moving around the other. In particular, the sort of curves produced by the pen depend on the following circumstances:

1. The relative size of the wheels A and B
2. The relative distance of the tracer T from the spindle E, and of that spindle from the axis X
3. Whether the wheel D is employed or not.

These factors are reflected in the tables presented later in the book.

DEVELOPMENT OF THE GEOMETRIC PEN

In discussing the Geometric Pen in his book, *A Treatise on Mathematical Drawing Instruments,* W.F. Stanley said, in 1866:

> We can but be struck with the simplicity of arrangement of the Geometric Pen, which produces a thousand varieties of ornamental figures in geometrical proportions, for the most part bearing so slight a resemblance to each other, that it is difficult to conceive that they can be the production of a single instrument.

A modified Geometric Pen was developed by Stanley and is illustrated in Figure 2. Stanley, who considered Suardi's pen "more as an amusing philosophical toy than as a mathematical instrument," claimed to have improved its general construction. He maintained that this enabled curves to be produced to any required size and "at the same time their variety is multiplied a hundredfold."

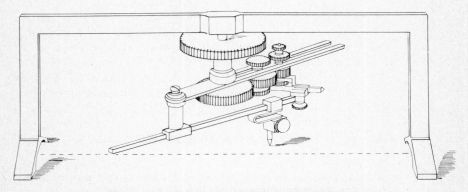

FIGURE 2   STANLEY'S IMPROVED GEOMETRIC PEN

A further refinement to the Geometric Pen was alluded to in 1878 by R.A. Proctor in *Treatise on the Cycloid:*

> Mr Perigal has invented, also, an ingenious instrument, called the kinescope (sold by Messrs. R. & J. Beck, of Cornhill), by which all forms of epicyclics can be occularly illustrated. A bright head is set revolving with great rapidity about a centre, itself revolving rapidly about a fixed centre, and by simple adjustment, any velocity-ratio can be given to the two motions, and thus any epicyclic traced out. The motions are so rapid that, owing to the persistence of luminous images on the retina, the whole curve is visible as if formed of bright wire.

Today, a children's toy known as a Spirograph, marketed by Toltoys, can produce some of the simple patterns of the Geometric Pen.

INVENTION OF THE GEOMETRIC LATHE

Needless to say, the Geometric Pen was of limited practical use, since it could only *draw* patterns on paper. Of greater use was the Geometric Lathe, which was capable of *engraving* geometric patterns.

Savory states:

> The purpose for which the [Geometric Lathe] is principally used is to cut fine lines on flat surfaces of wood, or metal, or ivory, or vulcanite. If a surface of African black wood is made very smooth, and a fine pattern with the lines very close barely scratched on it, it has a very pretty effect. If a pattern is cut rather deeper in black wood or vulcanite, and filled in with white lead, it is very pretty. But the use of the [lathe] is by no means confined to fine lines: you can cut to a considerable depth. You may glue one thin piece of wood on a piece of another colour and cut through the upper, showing the lower.

Invention of this lathe dates back at least to the publication of *Manuel du Tourneur* by L. Bergeron in 1816, which contains a full account with engravings and specimens of a "machine epicycloide." The examples given are designed with a view to inlaying the curve with strips of tortoise shell and do not include the fine engraving previously described.

During the nineteenth century, refinements to the Geometric Lathe were effected by several English gentlemen, notably W. Hartley and J.H. Ibbetson. However, professional jealousy seems to have hindered progress for some time. For example, Ibbetson asserted that he had

> never made any particular communication of the mechanism of the instrument but to four gentlemen, who gave me their word and honour, under their handwriting, that they would not divulge any part of it in any way whatever.

Even when books were published, it seems they were done so with reluctance. In dedicating his book to the Worshipful Master of the Turner's Guild, W.H. Northcott said:

> The useful measures of technical advancement inaugurated by the Turners Company and so warmly promoted by yourself, tend greatly to encourage artistic skill and honourable emulation amongst craftsmen; I trust that my attempt to expose the mysteries and secrets of the craft will not be considered treasonable.

In the period between 1851 and 1884 several books of limited edition were published on the operation of the Geometric Lathe and the patterns it could produce. The patterns in this book are some of the interesting patterns illustrated in the literature of this period.

APPLICATIONS OF THE GEOMETRIC LATHE

While the Geometric Lathe was used largely for recreational purposes, it did have some practical applications. In 1820 Ibbetson wrote an article entitled "Practical View of an Invention for the Better Protection of Notes Against Forgery."

We are not able to obtain much information in this regard. Neither, apparently, is the *New Scientist* magazine (22-29 December 1983), which reported that the Bank of England used a geometric drawing machine in the design of banknotes, but that "the Bank is unwilling either to demonstrate the machine or to send out free samples of its work."

However, a perusal of our $10 and $20 notes reveals numerous geometric designs obviously produced by mechanical means. No doubt banknotes of other countries contain similar geometric designs, evidencing contemporary use of the Geometric Lathe or similar instrument.

Today's computer screen is the perfect medium for reproducing geometric patterns. However, the more practically minded may use their plotter printers and follow the example of several readers of the *New Scientist* magazine, who reported using their harmonographs for decorating greeting cards, book jackets, letterheads, and other personalized stationery.

Visitors to London may be interested in inspecting Mr Perigal's Geometric Lathe or "compound geometric chuck" as well as his "kinescope." These instruments are on display at the South Kensington Museum. Also, the Society of Ornamental Turners holds exhibitions at this museum, demonstrating the use of the Geometric Lathe.

If you are interested in reading more about the history of the Geometric Lathe, you may refer to Martin Matthew's book *Engine Turning*, which is available through the Society of Ornamental Turners in London.

3 Plotting a Circle on the Computer Screen

Plotting the illustrated patterns on the computer screen requires initially putting the computer into the high-resolution graphics mode. The procedure for doing this varies between computers. This book uses hypothetical commands to select the high-resolution mode and to plot the points which generate a pattern.

The information at the back of this chapter will enable you to effect this on *current* models of Apple II, TRS-80 Color, Atari, BBC, Commodore 64, ZX Spectrum, IBM-PC, and Microbee computers. It would clearly be impossible to include specific information on all micros or, indeed, on earlier models of these computers. However, you should have little difficulty in converting the three or four hypothetical commands used, to suit your own computer, by referring to your respective user manual.

It is beyond the scope of this book to examine the mathematical aspects of generating ornamental patterns. However, some understanding will be obtained by consideration of the formula necessary to plot a circle.

At the risk of seeming tedious to mathematicians but in the interests of other readers, let us consider the set of parametric equations for representing mathematically a point on a circle. That is,

$$X = COS (A)$$
$$Y = SIN (A)$$

The terms Cos (A) and Sin (A) are explained in any elementary maths book. They are not explained here, purely because it is not necessary to understand them, only how to use them. Many drivers don't understand how their cars work, but they do understand how to drive them.

The following is the general form of a program necessary for the computer to plot a circle:

```
10   HCOLOR
20   FOR A = 0 TO 2*π STEP .1
30   X = 50*COS(A) + 100
40   Y = 50*SIN(A) + 100
50   PLOT X,Y
60   NEXT A
```

Let us now type this program into the computer and run it. Slight amendments may be required to the program as different computers have different commands or routines for high-resolution graphics plotting. As mentioned, you should read the appropriate section at the end of this chapter or your own computer manual.

In any event, we shall consider each program line in turn, in order to assist understanding.

This instruction or its equivalent puts the computer into a high-resolution graphics mode:

```
10   HCOLOR
```

This instruction determines the length of the program because it sets up a program loop:

```
20   FOR A = 0 TO 2*π STEP .1
```

If your computer does not have the symbol π on the keyboard, type its numerical equivalent: 3.14159.

You will note that if the program line is changed to:

```
20   FOR A = 0 TO π STEP .1
```

the computer will plot only half a circle. Whereas, if the line is changed to:

```
20   FOR A = 0 TO 4*π STEP .1
```

the computer will plot the same circle twice. You will see later that when you plot some detailed patterns, it is sometimes necessary to use the latter instruction for the computer to complete an entire pattern.

Let us now change the program line as follows:

```
20   FOR A = 0 TO 2*π STEP .2
```

You will note that the computer plots a circle with the dots farther apart. Alternatively, if you change the line to:

20   FOR A = 0 TO 2*π STEP .1

the computer plots a circle with the dots closer together.

There is an obvious trade-off here, between the degree of detail required to plot a pattern clearly and the time taken to plot it. The closer the dots, the more time it takes for the computer to complete the pattern.

As discussed earlier, this set of equations, with refinements, generates the circle:

30   X = 50*COS(A) + 100
40   Y = 50*SIN(A) + 100

The constant 50 determines the radius of the circle. This circle will just fit on a screen 100 units in height and width.

If your computer has a high-resolution screen smaller than 100 units in height or width, you will have to adjust the constant accordingly. A screen of, for example, 80 units in height will accommodate a circle with a radius of no more than 40.

The constant 100 in program lines 30 and 40 centers the circle in the middle of a screen of 200 units in height and 200 units in width.

If we have a computer with a screen 80 units in height by 120 units in width, the appropriate set of program lines to generate a circle which would just fit on the screen centered in the middle would be as follows:

30   X = 40*COS(A) + 60
40   Y = 40*SIN(A) + 40

This instruction directs the computer to print a dot on the screen at the point (x,y):

50   PLOT X,Y

You should refer to the appropriate section at the end of this chapter or your own user manual for the appropriate command or routine for your particular computer. Some computers use another parameter within this instruction which determines color or whether to plot a line or point.

The instruction:

60   NEXT A

directs the computer back in a loop to line 20. (Some computers do not require "A" to be typed in.)

You should now be able to generate a circle on your screen using the above program modified to suit your particular computer. If you are experiencing difficulties at this stage, recheck your computer manual to confirm the height and width of your high-resolution screen and the centering and radius of your circle. Experiment a little if necessary and discuss your problems with other computer operators.

PLOTTING A CIRCLE ON PAPER

In order to plot a circle on paper you will need an X–Y plotter printer. Such a printer uses a small ballpoint pen which draws a continuous line without lifting from the page after each individual point plotted. Resolution is therefore better than on the computer screen but this is not appreciable except with extremely detailed patterns such as Figure 603.

The program necessary to plot a circle will depend on the computer and printer used. You should consult your computer and printer user manuals in order to ascertain the correct routine for plotting with a printer. The general form of this program will of course be similar to that used at the start of this chapter.

INSTRUCTIONS FOR VARIOUS COMPUTERS

The following section provides instructions for various computers:

APPLE II COMPUTER

```
10   HGR 2
20   FOR A = 0 TO 2*3.14159 STEP .1
30   X = 50*COS(A) + 140
40   Y = 50*SIN(A) + 96
50   HPLOT X,Y
60   NEXT A
```

Line 10 set computer in full-screen high-resolution graphics mode. (The command HGR retains a text window at the bottom of the screen.)

Line 20 sets up program loop. (Insert numerical value of π, 3.14159, as the symbol is not represented on keyboard.)

Lines 30 and 40 center circle on (280*192) screen.

Line 50 plots dot at point (x,y).

Line 60 returns loop to line 20.

ATARI 600XL and 800XL COMPUTER

```
 8   GRAPHICS 8 + 16
 9   SETCOLOR 2,0,0
10   COLOR 1
20   FOR A = 0 TO 2*3.14159 STEP .1
30   X = 50*COS(A) + 140
40   Y = 50*SIN(A) + 96
50   PLOT X,Y
60   NEXT A
70   GOTO 70
```

Line 8 sets computer in full-screen high-resolution graphics mode.

Lines 9 and 10 set computer to plot white on black background.

Line 20 sets up program loop. (Insert numerical value of π, 3.14159, as the symbol is not represented on keyboard.)

Lines 30 and 40 center circle on (280*192) screen.

Line 50 plots dot at point (x,y).

Line 60 returns loop to line 20.

Line 70 freezes picture on screen.

BBC COMPUTER

```
10   MODE 4
20   FOR A = 0 TO 2*3.14159 STEP .1
30   X = 50*COS(A) + 640
40   Y = 50*SIN(A) + 512
50   PLOT 69,X,Y
60   NEXT A
```

Line 10 sets computer in full-screen high-resolution graphics mode.

Line 20 sets up program loop. (Insert numerical value of π, 3.14159, as the symbol is not represented on keyboard.)

Lines 30 and 40 center circle on (1280*1024) screen.

Line 50 plots dot at point (x,y).

Line 60 returns loop to line 20.

In view of the different screen dimensions you will find it better to use coefficient values (in this case, 50) as much as four times larger than those given in this book.

COMMODORE 64 COMPUTER

```
 7   BASE = 2*4096: POKE 53272, PEEK (53272) OR 8
 8   POKE 53265, PEEK (53265) OR 32
 9   FOR I = BASE TO BASE + 7999: POKE I,0 : NEXT
10   FOR I = 1024 TO 2023: POKE I,3 : NEXT
20   FOR A = 0 TO 2*π STEP .1
30   X = 50*COS(A) + 160
40   Y = 50*SIN(A) + 100
50   CH = INT(X/8)
51   RO = INT(Y/8)
52   LN = YAND7
53   BY = BASE + RO*320 + 8*CH + LN
54   BI = 7 − (XAND7)
55   POKEBY,PEEK(BY) OR (2↑BI)
60   NEXT A
70   GOTO 70
```

Lines 7 and 8 set computer in full-screen high-resolution graphics mode.

Line 9 clears screen.

Line 10 sets screen to plot black on yellow background.

Line 20 sets up program loop.

Lines 30 and 40 center circle on (320*200) screen.

Lines 50 to 55 plot dot at point (x,y).

Line 60 returns loop to line 20.

Line 70 freezes picture on screen.

It takes approximately 30 seconds to clear the high-resolution screen before plotting commences.

In view of the detail involved in this plotting routine, you may choose to record it on tape or disk for future use, rather than having to retype it each time. Alternatively, you may choose to use the Superexpander or Simons BASIC Cartridge (see next listing).

COMMODORE 64 WITH SUPEREXPANDER CARTRIDGE

```
10   GRAPHIC 2,1
20   FOR A = 0 TO 2*π STEP .1
30   X = 50*COS(A) + 160
40   Y = 50*SIN(A) + 100
50   DRAW 1,X,Y
60   NEXT A
70   GOTO 70
```

Line 10 sets computer in full-screen high-resolution graphics mode.

Line 20 sets up program loop.

Lines 30 and 40 center circle on (320*200) screen.

Line 50 plots dot at point (x,y).

Line 60 returns loop to line 20.

Line 70 freezes picture on screen.

IBM-PC

```
10   SCREEN 2,0,0
20   FOR A = 0 TO 2*3.14159 STEP .1
30   X = 50*COS(A) + 320
40   Y = 50/2*SIN(A) + 100
50   PSET(X,Y)
60   NEXT A
```

Line 10 sets computer in full-screen high-resolution graphics mode.

Line 20 sets up program loop. (Insert numerical value of π, 3.14159, as the symbol is not represented on keyboard.)

Lines 30 and 40 center circle on (640*200) screen.

Line 50 plots dot at point (x,y).

Line 60 returns loop to line 20.

Check that the computer you are using is modified for high-resolution graphics as this is not a standard feature on the PC.

A space must be left after each command word (except where brackets are used as in line 50).

The coefficient in line 40 must always be divided by 2. This principle applies to other coefficients of Sine used later. For example, the function used to plot some detailed patterns in this book is shown as:

```
30   X = R*COS(A) + S*COS(N*A) + T*COS(M*A) + 100
40   Y = R*SIN(A) + S*SIN(N*A) + T*SIN(M*A) + 100
```

For the IBM-PC use the following function:

```
30   X = R*COS(A) + S*COS(N*A) + T*COS(M*A) + 320
40   Y = R/2*SIN(A) + S/2*SIN(N*A) + T/2*SIN(M*A) + 100
```

MICROBEE COMPUTER

```
10   HIRES
20   FOR A1 = 0 TO 2*3.14159 STEP .1
30   X = INT(50*COS(A1)) + 256
40   Y = INT(50/1.5*SIN(A1)) + 128
50   SET X,Y
60   NEXT A1
```

Line 10 sets computer in full-screen high-resolution graphics mode.

Line 20 sets up program loop. (Insert numerical value of π, 3.14159, as the symbol is not represented on keyboard.)

Lines 30 and 40 center circle on (512*256) screen.

Line 50 plots dot at point (x,y).

Line 60 returns loop to line 20.

Always use the coefficient A1 and not A. Similarly, later in the book, coefficients R1, S1, T1, N1, and M1 must be used, and not R, S, T, N, and M.

Lines 30 and 40 require use of the expression INT, as the SET command in line 50 recognizes only integral values of x and y. Be careful to use brackets as above so that the entire parametric function is enclosed within them.

The coefficient 50 in line 40 must always be divided by 1.5. This principle applies to other coefficients of Sine used later. For example, the function used to plot some detailed patterns in this book is shown as:

```
30   X = R*COS(A) + S*COS(N*A)+ T*COS(M*A) + 100
40   Y = R*SIN(A) + S*SIN(N*A) + T*SIN(M*A) + 100
```

For the Microbee, use the following function:

```
30   X = INT(R1*COS(A1) + S1*COS(N1*A1) +
         T1*COS(M1*A1)) + 256
40   Y = INT(R1/1.5*SIN(A1) + S1/1.5*SIN(N1*A1) +
         T1/1.5*SIN(M1*A1)) + 128
```

TRS-80 COLOR COMPUTER

```
 8   PMODE 4,1
 9   PCLS
10   SCREEN 1,0
20   FOR A = 0 TO 2*3.14159 STEP .1
30   X = 50*COS(A) + 128
40   Y = 50*SIN(A) + 96
50   PSET(X,Y,1)
60   NEXT A
70   GOTO 70
```

Line 8 sets computer in full-screen high-resolution graphics mode.

Line 9 clears screen.

Line 10 sets computer to plot white on black background.

Line 20 sets up program loop. (Insert numerical value of π, 3.14159, as the symbol is not represented on keyboard.)

Lines 30 and 40 center circle on (256*192) screen.

Line 50 plots dot at point (x,y).

Line 60 returns loop to line 20.

Line 70 freezes picture on screen.

ZX SPECTRUM COMPUTER

```
20   FOR A = 0 TO 2*3.14159 STEP .1
30   X = 50*COS(A) + 128
40   Y = 50*SIN(A) + 88
50   PLOT X,Y
60   NEXT A
```

Line 20 sets up program loop.

Lines 30 and 40 center circle on (256*176) screen.

Line 50 sets computer in full-screen high-resolution graphics mode. It also plots dot at point (x,y).

Line 60 returns loop to line 20.

4 Plotting Epicyclic Patterns

We are now in a position to summarize the preceding two chapters:

   1. The Geometric Pen traces a curve or pattern which is the path of a pen on the circumference of a secondary wheel, rolling around a primary or fixed wheel.
   2. The program required for the computer to plot a circle is of the general form:

```
10   HCOLOR
20   FOR A = 0 TO 2*π STEP .1
30   X = R*COS(A) + 100
40   Y = R*SIN(A) + 100
50   PLOT X,Y
60   NEXT A
```

where R is a constant whose numerical value is equal to the radius of the circle.

   From this, you may deduce that the program for plotting the pattern of the Geometric Pen, being based on the movement of two wheels or circles, will be of the following form:

```
10   HCOLOR
20   FOR A = 0 TO 2*π STEP .01
30   X = R*COS(A) + S*COS(N*A) + 100
40   Y = R*SIN(A) + S*SIN(N*A) + 100
50   PLOT X,Y
60   NEXT A
```

22

where R and S are constants whose numerical values are equal to the radiuses of the fixed and rolling circles respectively. (The significance of N will be discussed in the next chapter.)

Let us now type the preceding program into the computer, modifying it if necessary as for plotting the circle, as previously discussed. Before you run the program it will be necessary to insert values for R, S, and N. Accordingly, type in the following line:

15   R = 50 : S = 50 : N = 9

and run the program. You should end up with the pattern in Figure 3.

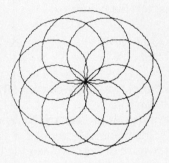

FIGURE 3

This pattern may be made larger or smaller in a similar manner to the circle, as discussed in the previous chapter. However, it is necessary to change the values of both R and S, but maintaining the same proportion between them. For example, the following program lines will generate successively smaller but identical patterns:

15   R = 40 : S = 40 : N = 9
15   R = 30 : S = 30 : N = 9
15   R = 20 : S = 20 : N = 9

Note that it is necessary to change only the values of R and S in proportion, but not the value of N. In fact the sum of (R + S) is equal to the radius of the curve or pattern, in the same way that R is equal to the radius of the circle previously described.

Accordingly if you have a computer whose screen height in high resolution is, say, 200, then it will not be possible to fit a pattern on the screen if the sum of R and S exceeds 100. These coefficients will need to be scaled down as previously outlined.

Most coefficients given in this book are based on a computer having a 160 x 160 high-resolution screen. If your computer has, for example, a 200 x 200 screen, most values for R and S given in this book could be increased by 25 percent and still fit the screen. But remember it is not necessary for you to calculate this each time. Let the computer do it for you. For example, set up your standard program lines as follows:

```
30   X = 1.25*R*COS(A) + 1.25*S*COS(N*A) + 100
40   Y = 1.25*R*SIN(A) + 1.25*S*SIN(N*A) + 100
```

Another method of obtaining the largest possible pattern would be to insert additional program lines, such as:

```
16   R = R + 1: S = S + 1/R
17   IF R + S < 98 THEN 16
```

Now you can forget about having to convert all the data in this book. The computer will do it for you.

One further point of note is the sign of the coefficient N. As will be seen in the next chapter, the patterns generated for the same value of N, but with different sign (positive or negative), are significantly different. In nineteenth century literature such patterns are referred to as companion curves because of their identical lathe settings.

HISTORY OF EPICYCLIC CURVES OR PATTERNS

The patterns traced out by use of the previous program are known by mathematicians generally as "epicyclic" curves or "epicycloids." An epicycloid is the path traced out by a point on the circumference of a secondary circle (known as the "epicyclic" circle) which rolls without sliding around a primary or fixed circle (known as the "deferent" circle). You will recall that the movement of the Geometric Pen is consistent with this definition.

Epicyclics played a great part in ancient astronomy. If we ignore the eccentricities and inclinations of the planetary orbits, the Sun may be regarded as describing a circle around the Earth, and any other planet as describing a circle on the same plane about the Sun. The path of the planet relative to the Earth is therefore epicyclic or looping. This was the accepted view of planetary motion from the time of Ptolemy (second century A.D.) to the sixteenth century, when it was gradually superseded by the simpler method of describing the phenomena discovered by Copernicus.

Ptolemy's Theory of Planetary Epicyclics was an ingenious way of describing an apparent retrograde or looping motion of planets as seen from Earth. The patterns in Figures 4, 5, 6, 7, 8, and 9, taken from R.A. Proctor's book *Treatise on the Cycloid,* are based on astronomical data and represent the approximate epicyclic curves traced by the planets, with reference to the Earth regarded as fixed.

These patterns can be plotted on the computer by inserting the following program lines in the general program given at the start of this chapter:

Mercury (Figure 4)

```
15   R = 50 : S = 20 : N = 29/7
20   FOR A = 0 TO 14*π STEP .05
```

Venus (Figure 5)

```
15   R = 50 : S = 35 : N = 13/8
20   FOR A = 0 TO 16*π STEP .05
```

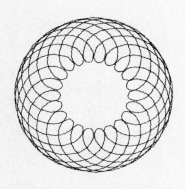

FIGURE 4 MERCURY

119,653

FIGURE 5 VENUS

Mars (Figure 6)

15   R = 51 : S = 34 : N = 2
20   FOR A = 0 TO 2*π STEP .05

Jupiter (Figure 7)

15   R = 50 : S = 10 : N = 12
20   FOR A = 0 TO 2*π STEP .025

Saturn (Figure 8)

15   R = 57 : S = 6 : N = 59/2
20   FOR A = 0 TO 4*π STEP .01

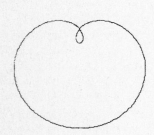

FIGURE 6 MARS

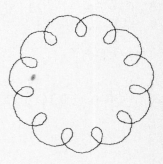

FIGURE 7 JUPITER

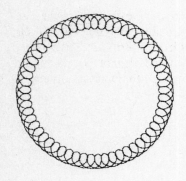

FIGURE 8 SATURN

FIGURE 9 URANUS

Uranus (Figure 9)

```
15   R = 85.5 : S = 4.5 : N = 85
20   FOR A = 0 TO 2*π STEP .005
```

In view of the above, it is not surprising that epicyclic curves are also referred to as "planetary" curves.

You will realise that the preceding patterns are all plotted from an overhead perspective, looking down on the Earth at the center. Of course, an observer on Earth will have an entirely different perspective, looking outwards from the middle of the system. Accordingly he will only see part of the pattern (over a period of time), being a looping arc in the sky. Interested readers may care to refer to J. Bronowski's book *The Ascent of Man* (BBC), for a delayed photograph of the apparent looping paths of the planets.

While you may see some coincidence between the ancient Greek theory of astronomy and the motion of the Geometric Pen, it is suggested that this is more than accidental. For centuries man has sought to devise instruments displaying planetary motion. As early as 1350, an astronomical clock was invented by Giovanni de Dondi of Padua, Italy, simulating the epicyclic or looping motion of the planets. (The original of this clock has not survived, but a reconstruction made from de Dondi's working drawings now stands in the Smithsonian Institution in Washington, D.C.)

Whether Suardi was aware of the de Dondi clock, or whether he developed the Geometric Pen independently, does not concern us. However, the reference in the title of his book to *Curve antichi e moderne* suggests that Suardi, like de Dondi, intended the instrument to simulate the motion of the planets as postulated by the ancient Greeks. In contrast to de Dondi, however, Suardi realised the instrument could generate other interesting patterns.

Ironically it would seem that such patterns, expanded and developed by the Victorians in the nineteenth century and illustrated throughout this book, are all predicated on the ancient Greek theory of astronomy. Perhaps the celestial harmony referred to by the ancient Greeks as the "Music of the Spheres" should be paraphrased in the present context to the "Symmetry of the Spheres," in view of the perfect aesthetic lines of the patterns generated.

5 Plotting Consecutive Epicyclic Patterns

Let us now consider in more detail the properties of epicyclic or "planetary" curves; that is, those curves or patterns generated by the computer from the following general program:

```
10   HCOLOR
15   R = :S = :N =
20   FOR A = 0 TO 2*π STEP .1
30   X = R*COS(A) + S*COS(N*A) + 100
40   Y = R*SIN(A) + S*SIN(N*A) + 100
50   PLOT X,Y
60   NEXT A
```

Bazley wrote:

> When an amateur of the Art of Turning adds to his apparatus the [Geometric Lathe] he will probably, if at all prone to scientific dabblings, soon desire to know something of the laws upon which the action of such an instrument depends, and will not be contented with admiring the facility with which, by haphazard adjustments, this species of ornamentation can be applied to the decoration of plane surfaces.

The shape of an epicyclic pattern depends on the values given to the coefficients R, S, and N in the line 15 of the preceding program. R and S are always positive. N may be positive or negative and has the most influence of the three in determining the character of the curve.

In this chapter, we shall consider patterns generated from integral values (whole numbers) of N only. For reasons which will become apparent in the next chapter, such patterns are known as "consecutive" epicyclic patterns.

Let us begin by considering the development of patterns generated from a positive value of N, say N = 5. The respective values of R and S are as follows:

Figure 10	$R = 75 : S = R/N^2 = 3$	Pattern is rectilinear.
Figure 11	$R = 65 : S = R/N = 13$	Pattern is cusped.
Figure 12	$R = 56 : S = 24$	Loops appear.
Figure 13	$R = 44 : S = 36$	Loops touch.
Figure 14	$R = 40 : S = 40$	Loops pass through center.
Figure 15	$R = 30 : S = 50$	Loops intersect.

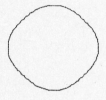

FIGURE 10

FIGURE 11

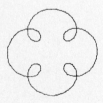

FIGURE 12

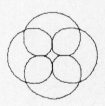

FIGURE 13

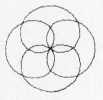

FIGURE 14

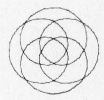

FIGURE 15

Let us consider the development of patterns generated from another positive value of N, say N = 7. The respective values of R and S are as follows:

Figure 16   R = 78.4 : S = R/N^2 = 1.6   Pattern is rectilinear.
Figure 17   R = 70   : S = R/N = 10   Pattern is cusped.
Figure 18   R = 56   : S = 24   Loops appear.
Figure 19   R = 50   : S = 30   Loops touch.
Figure 20   R = 40   : S = 40   Loops pass through center.
Figure 21   R = 32   : S = 48   Loops intersect.

FIGURE 16

FIGURE 17

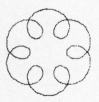

FIGURE 18

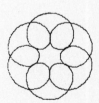

FIGURE 19

FIGURE 20

FIGURE 21

Let us consider the development of the patterns generated from a negative value of N, say N = −2. The respective values of R and S are as follows:

Figure 22 R = 64 : S = R/N² = 16   Pattern is rectilinear.
Figure 23 R = 54 : S = R/N = 27   Pattern is cusped.
Figure 24 R = 48 : S = 32   Loops appear.
Figure 25 R = 40 : S = 40   Loops pass through center.
Figure 26 R = 30 : S = 50   Loops intersect.
Figure 27 R = 10 : S = 70   Loops intersect.

In this case no touching or side contact of the loops occurs, as is evident from the course of the curve.

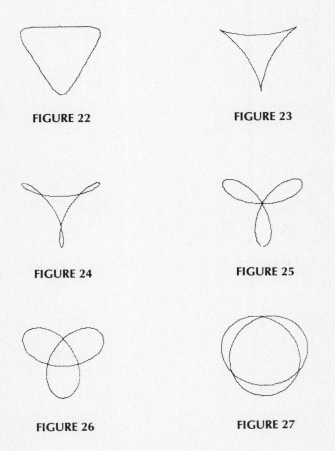

FIGURE 22   FIGURE 23

FIGURE 24   FIGURE 25

FIGURE 26   FIGURE 27

Let us consider the development of patterns generated from another negative value of N, say N = −4. The respective values of R and S are as follows:

Figure 28 R = 75 : S = R/N² = 4.7   Pattern is rectilinear.
Figure 29 R = 64 : S = R/N = 16   Pattern is cusped.
Figure 30 R = 54 : S = 26   Loops appear.
Figure 31 R = 42 : S = 38   Loops touch.
Figure 32 R = 40 : S = 40   Loops pass through center.
Figure 33 R = 30 : S = 50   Loops intersect.

FIGURE 28

FIGURE 29

FIGURE 30

FIGURE 31

FIGURE 32

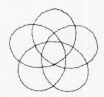

FIGURE 33

INTERPRETATION OF PATTERN DEVELOPMENTS

A close inspection of the previous groups of patterns will reveal the following Rules of Pattern Development.

Rules Concerning N

Rules concerning N are as follows:

1. Where N is positive, the loops are internal.
2. Where N is negative, the loops are external.
3. Where N is positive, the number of loops is equal to the numerical value of $N - 1$.
4. Where N is negative, the number of loops is equal to the numerical value of $N + 1$.

Rules Concerning R and S

Rules concerning R and S are as follows:

1. Where $S = R/N^2$, the pattern is rectilinear.
2. Where $S = R/N$, the pattern is cusped.
3. Where $S = R$, the loops of pattern pass through center.

Several other rules concerning R and S derive from the fact that R is the radius of the fixed circle and S is the radius of the epicyclic circle. These rules are:

4. $R + S$ is equal to the radius of the curve or pattern.
5. $R - S$ is equal to the shortest distance of the curve or pattern from the center. This may be restated in that as R and S approach one another, the curve or pattern approaches the center. (You will note that rule 3 above is a special case of this principle.) Conversely as R and S diverge, the curve or pattern recedes from the center.
6. Rules 4 and 5 taken together indicate that the whole of the curve or pattern lies within the annular space or ring, whose maximum width is $R + S$ and whose minimum width is $R - S$, that is, $2*S$. (In fact common sense would suggest that the width of the ring would be equal to the diameter of the epicyclic circle.)

Rules Concerning R, S, and N

It is possible to generate the same pattern by:

- Interposing the values of R and S.
- Substituting $1/N$ for N, or $-1/N$ for $-N$.

For example, the following sets of coefficients will plot the pattern in Figure 34:

15   R = 60 : S = 20 : N = 9
15   R = 20 : S = 60 : N = 1/9

In the latter case, the step size will need to be increased nine times that of the former, as follows:

20   FOR A = 0 TO 18*π STEP .02

Reasons for this are explained in the next chapter where we deal with fractional values of N.
Bazley wrote:

> It may now be stated that there are two ways of describing the same simple curve, whether its loops be consecutive or circulating and whether they be internal or external. It does not follow however that both ways will be equally eligible . . . The curve is more easily traced [by the Geometric Lathe] when the eccentricity of the slide rest [represented by the coefficient S] is less than that of the chuck slide [represented by the coefficient R].

Fortunately, as stated in the introduction, the personal computer does not suffer the same physical limitations as the Geometric Lathe. The information is presented here to eliminate any confusion readers may have in generating the same pattern with different sets of coefficients.

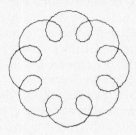

FIGURE 34

It is possible to calculate algebraically the values of R and S for each value of N, such that the loops touch, as in Figures 13, 19, 25, and 31. The rule involves a knowledge of differential calculus and is beyond the scope of this book. However the following table may assist readers interested in plotting such patterns. It sets out the respective values of R and S to two decimal places, for different values (positive and negative) of N. You may estimate values of R and S for larger values of N by extrapolation.

±N	R/S	R	S
3	1	40.00	40.00
4	1.09	41.70	38.30
5	1.25	44.44	35.56
6	1.43	47.15	32.85
7	1.63	49.59	30.41
8	1.83	51.76	28.24
9	2.03	53.61	26.39
10	2.24	55.36	24.64
11	2.45	56.87	23.13
12	2.66	58.13	21.87
13	2.87	59.33	20.67
14	3.09	60.44	19.56
15	3.31	61.44	18.56
16	3.53	62.34	17.56
17	3.75	63.16	16.84
18	3.97	63.90	16.10
19	4.20	64.62	15.38
20	4.43	65.27	14.73

6 Plotting Circulating Epicyclic Patterns

Let us now consider the properties of epicyclic curves, where N is fractional. Again we shall use the general program:

```
10  HCOLOR
15  R = : S = : N =
20  FOR A = 0 TO 2*π STEP .1
30  X = R*COS(A) + S*COS(N*A) + 100
40  Y = R*SIN(A) + S*SIN(N*A) + 100
50  PLOT X,Y
60  NEXT A
```

Let us begin by selecting a positive value for N, say N = 9/2. In this case it is necessary to change line 20 as follows:

```
20  FOR A = 0 TO 4*π STEP .1
```

The reason for this will be apparent to anyone attempting to execute the program without making this adjustment. Only half the pattern will be reproduced by the computer. This is because for a value of N of 9/2, pattern development is such that a point on the epicyclic or rolling circle only returns to its original position after two rotations around the fixed circle. The adjustment to line 20 lengthens the program accordingly.

Similarly for a value of N of, say, 10/3, pattern development is such that the point on the epicyclic or rolling circle will only return to its original position after three rotations around the fixed circle. It is therefore necessary to adjust line 20 to lengthen the original program three times as follows:

20   FOR A = 0 TO 6*π STEP .1

Corresponding adjustments to line 20 are required for other fractional values of N. For example, if N = 21/4, the adjustment required will be:

20   FOR A = 0 TO 8*π STEP .1

You should note that in applying this rule the fractional value of N must always be in its lowest terms. For example, 21/4 and not 42/8.

As you increase the program length, you will find that the space between points plotted on the computer screen increases. Accordingly it may be necessary to reduce the step size. For example:

20   FOR A = 0 TO 18*π STEP .025

The fact that, where N is fractional, the epicyclic wheel must rotate a number of times around the fixed wheel before a pattern was completed led Victorians to term such patterns as "circulating." It can be seen that, with these patterns, loops are not plotted consecutively but at every other or greater intervals. This tends to give a rather pleasing overlapping effect, as Bazley states:

> Generally speaking, the curves with loops formed consecutively are far inferior in interest and variety to those called "circulating" where the loops occur alternatively or at wider intervals.

Let us now revert to our example where N = 9/2. The same rules apply regarding the values of R and S as for simple patterns. However, the number of loops generated is equal to the numerator minus the denominator, that is, 9 − 2 = 7 in this case.

You will note that in generating this pattern, loops are not plotted consecutively as with simple patterns. They are plotted alternately (i.e. plotting one, missing one, etc.), the loops missed being plotted on the second rotation of the epicyclic or rolling circle.

Figure 35 $R = 60 : S = R/N^2$ (nearly) $= 3$ Pattern is rectilinear.
Figure 36 $R = 50 : S = R/N$ (nearly) $= 11$ Pattern is cusped.
Figure 37 $R = 40 : S = 20$ Loops appear.
Figure 38 $R = 30 : S = 30$ Loops pass through center.
Figure 39 $R = 20 : S = 40$ Loops intersect.
Figure 40 $R = 10 : S = 50$ Loops intersect.

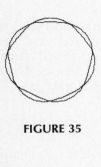

FIGURE 35

FIGURE 36

FIGURE 37

FIGURE 38

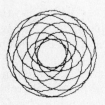

FIGURE 39

FIGURE 40

If we now take N = 10/3, you will note that every third loop is plotted on the first rotation of the epicycle around the fixed circle similarly on the second and third rotations until the pattern is completed. Again the number of loops generated is 10 − 3 = 7.

Figure 41   R = 55.1 : S = R/N² = 4.9   Pattern is rectilinear.
Figure 42   R = 46.2 : S = R/N = 13.8   Pattern is cusped.
Figure 43   R = 40   : S = 20   Loops appear.
Figure 44   R = 30   : S = 30   Loops pass through center.
Figure 45   R = 20   : S = 40   Loops intersect.
Figure 46   R = 10   : S = 50   Loops intersect.

FIGURE 41

FIGURE 42

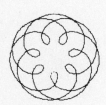

FIGURE 43

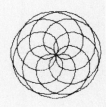

FIGURE 44

FIGURE 45

FIGURE 46

If we select negative fractional values of N, say $N = -11/6$, you will note the same principles apply regarding the values of R and S as for simple patterns. However, the number of loops generated is equal to the numerator plus the denominator, that is, $11 + 6 = 17$ loops or cusps, which are plotted every sixth one at a time. In contrast to positive fractional values of N, loops and cusps are now external.

Figure 47 $R = 46.3 : S = R/N^2 = 13.7$ Pattern is rectilinear.
Figure 48 $R = 38.8 : S = R/N = 21.2$ Pattern is cusped.
Figure 49 $R = 33$ $: S = 27$ Loops appear.
Figure 50 $R = 30$ $: S = 30$ Loops pass through center.
Figure 51 $R = 20$ $: S = 40$ Loops intersect.
Figure 52 $R = 10$ $: S = 50$ Loops intersect.

FIGURE 47

FIGURE 48

FIGURE 49

FIGURE 50

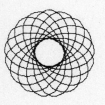

FIGURE 51

FIGURE 52

Let us select one further negative fractional value of N, say N = −12/5, to confirm the same development of curves occurs. You will note that the computer generates 12 + 5 = 17 loops or cusps, which are plotted every fifth one at a time.

Figure 53	R = 51.1 : S = R/N² = 8.9	Pattern is rectilinear.
Figure 54	R = 42.4 : S = R/N = 17.6	Pattern is cusped.
Figure 55	R = 35 : S = 25	Loops appear.
Figure 56	R = 30 : S = 30	Loops pass through center.
Figure 57	R = 20 : S = 40	Loops intersect.
Figure 58	R = 10 : S = 50	Loops intersect.

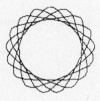

FIGURE 53

FIGURE 54

FIGURE 55

FIGURE 56

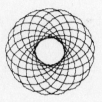

FIGURE 57

FIGURE 58

INTERPRETATION OF PATTERN DEVELOPMENT

A close inspection of the previous groups of patterns will reveal Rules of Pattern Development similar to those previously stated. In fact the following rules are a more general statement of the previous rules, and apply to all values of N, whether positive or negative, integral or fractional.

Rules Concerning N

Rules concerning N are as follows:

1. Where $N > 0$, the loops are internal.
2. Where $N < 0$, the loops are external.
3. Where $N > 0$, the number of loops is equal to the numerator minus the denominator.
4. Where $N < 0$, the number of loops is equal to the numerator plus the denominator.

Rules Concerning R and S

Rules concerning R and S are as follows:

1. Where $S = R/N^2$, the pattern is rectilinear.
2. Where $S = R/N$, the pattern is cusped.
3. Where $S = R$, the loops of pattern pass through center.
4. $R + S$ is equal to the maximum radius of the pattern.
5. $R - S$ is equal to the minimum radius of the pattern.
6. The entire pattern lies within annular space, whose width is $2*S$.

Rules Concerning R, S, and N

The same pattern can be generated by:

- Interposing the values of R and S
- Substituting $1/N$ for N, or $-1/N$ for $-N$.

If you have managed all this so far, you should have little difficulty with the patterns that follow. At this stage, you may choose to read progressively through the next chapter. However, if you are more impatient, you may choose to proceed directly to Chapter 8 and read how to plot the interesting patterns illustrated there. It is not necessary to absorb the detail of the next chapter before proceeding to Chapter 8. You may prefer to peruse Chapter 7 at a subsequent reading.

7 Plotting Detailed Epicyclic Patterns

We are now in a position to embellish some of the patterns we have generated on the computer.

In engraving such patterns, it appears that the Victorians often used the Geometric Lathe to produce successively deeper cuts, giving a three-dimensional or relief effect. Savory states:

> The [Geometric Lathe] has often been accused of being an instrument capable of producing fine scratches. Never was there a greater mistake . . . You may readily take a cut an eighth of an inch deep and wide at once and you may continue to the full depth of the drill. The step drills make most beautiful patterns; these cannot of course be represented by printing, but by means of a drill with a square end you can cut out figures . . . in relief in a succession of steps.

While we cannot produce the same three-dimensional effect on the computer screen, we can produce a similar effect by plotting successive expansions in different colors. How this is done will depend on the computer being used, but the principle involved is to link the changing value of R or S with the color plotting command. This will differ between computers as will the numbers of colors available for selection. An explanation follows Figure 59.

EXPANSIONS OF PATTERNS

The following patterns are all generated by modifying the general program for epicyclic curves:

```
10   HCOLOR
15   R =  : S =  : N =
20   FOR A = 0 TO 2*π STEP .05
30   X = R*COS(A) + S*COS(N*A) + 100
40   Y = R*SIN(A) + S*SIN(N*A) + 100
50   PLOT X,Y
60   NEXT A
```

Consecutive Epicyclic Patterns

Let us begin by plotting the same pattern in successively larger sizes, as in Figure 59.

FIGURE 59

The program necessary to generate this pattern involves two loops as against one before. The following lines need to be inserted in the general program:

```
14   N = 9
15   FOR R = 27 TO 81 STEP 9
16   S = R/9
70   NEXT R
```

You will note that line 16 maintains the relationship $S = R/N$. As outlined in Chapters 4 and 5, observance of this rule ensures that the loops of each successive pattern are cusped.

The program is designed to plot the same pattern for the following successive values of R and S:

R = 27, 36, 45, . . ., 81
S = 3, 4, 5, . . ., 9

You will recall from an earlier chapter that you can increase or decrease the size of a pattern by increasing or decreasing the size of R and S (but not N) in proportion. This is achieved by the loop generated by the lines 15 and 70.

You will note in running this program on a computer screen that the distance between dots increases as the pattern expands. Accordingly, for this and similar expanding patterns, some detail is lost. This problem can be overcome by a simple adjustment to the program linking the step size with the pattern size; for example:

20   FOR A = 0 TO 2*π STEP .05/(R/27)

In this case the step size will decrease from .05 to .017 as the pattern size increases.

A similar principle can be adopted to generate a different color for each successive expansion of the pattern. For example, if plotting color is determined by a parameter within the plot command, the program line:

50   PLOT X,Y, (R/9 – 27)

will generate a different dot color each time R increases by the step size of 9. You should consult your user manual in this regard, to ascertain the exact location of the color plotting parameter for your computer.

Circulating Epicyclic Patterns

Figure 59 was a consecutive pattern, but more interesting designs can be obtained from circulating patterns, as in Figure 60, which is achieved by inserting the following lines in the general program outlined at the start of this chapter:

FIGURE 60

```
14  N = -7/3
15  FOR R = 28 TO 88 STEP 12
16  S = 3/7*R
20  FOR A = 0 TO 6*π STEP .05/(R/28)
70  NEXT R
```

As with the previous pattern you will note that line 16 maintains the relationship S = R/N. As outlined in Chapters 4 and 5, observance of this rule ensures that the loops of each successive pattern are cusped.

In experimenting you may find that some similar circulating patterns are more appealing than others. For example, in the patterns in Figures 61 and 62, both have 19 external loops, but the center of Figure 61 is more cluttered and the loops are less appealing than in Figure 62.

In Figure 61, the relevant program lines are:

```
14  N = -14/5
15  FOR R = 27.5 TO 55 STEP 5.5
16  S = 7/11*R
20  FOR A = 0 TO 10*π STEP .05
70  NEXT R
```

In Figure 62, the relevant program lines are:

```
14  N = -12/7
15  FOR R = 27 TO 51 STEP 6
16  S = R - 6
20  FOR A = 0 TO 14*π STEP .05
```

FIGURE 61   **FIGURE 62**

You will note that in Figure 61 the pattern recurs every five loops. In Figure 62, the pattern recurs every seven loops. In Figure 61 the ratio R/S is constant. In Figure 62 the ratio (R − S) is constant.

It is readily apparent that you can experiment indefinitely along these lines to produce interesting patterns.

Other Pattern Developments

Let us now consider the effect of increasing the size of R, while holding S constant as in the patterns in Figures 63 and 64.

In Figure 63, the pattern is achieved by inserting the following lines in the general program outlined at the start of this chapter:

```
14   S = 11 : N = 7
15   FOR R = 17 TO 77 STEP 5
20   FOR A = 0 TO 2*π STEP .025
70   NEXT R
```

In Figure 64, the relevant program lines are:

```
14   S = 15 : N = −5
15   FOR R = 25 TO 75 STEP 5
20   FOR A = 0 TO 2*π STEP .025
70   NEXT R
```

FIGURE 63   **FIGURE 64**

You can see in the above programs that with each successive pattern the relationship $S = R/N$ is progressively approached. It is finally reached with the last (largest) pattern whose loops, in accordance with the rule outlined in Chapters 4 and 5, are therefore cusped.

You may be interested in comparing Figures 63 and 64 with Figures 65 and 66. Figures 63 and 64 are simple patterns (N is a positive integer), whereas Figures 65 and 66 are circulating (N being a positive fraction).

In Figure 65, the relevant program lines are:

```
14   S = 11 : N = 11/2
15   FOR R = 20 TO 80 STEP 10
20   FOR A = 0 TO 4*π STEP .025
70   NEXT R
```

In Figure 66, the relevant program lines are:

```
14   S = 24 : N = 21/4
15   FOR R = 60 TO 75 STEP 5
20   FOR A = 0 TO 8*π STEP .025
70   NEXT R
```

The differing effect of Figures 65 and 66 is due to the different ways in which the loops are developed. In Figure 65, loops are plotted alternatively (every second loop in turn). In Figure 66, loops are plotted every fourth loop in turn. It can be seen from these patterns that where loops are not plotted consecutively, the pattern becomes increasingly cluttered.

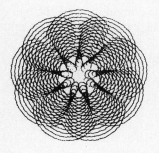

FIGURE 65

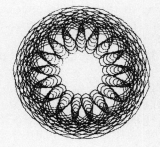

FIGURE 66

Let us now look at the effect of increasing the size of S, while holding R constant as in Figure 67. However, you will appreciate that this method is satisfactory only for low values of S. From the table at the end of Chapter 5, you will see that where R/S = 2.45 (i.e. S = 24.49 in this instance), the loops will touch. For higher values of S therefore, the cluttered effect will persist, as loops overlap one another.

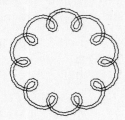

FIGURE 67

The relevant lines to be inserted in the general program are:

```
14   R = 60 : N = 11
15   FOR S = 10 TO 15 STEP 5
20   FOR A = 0 TO 2*π STEP .0125
70   NEXT S
```

This variation to some extent avoids the cluttered effect characteristic of Figures 65 and 66.

ROTATION OF PATTERNS

Victorian Geometric Lathe engravers would have achieved this effect by rotating the fixed wheel after each complete revolution of the epicyclic wheel. This effect can be achieved in a similar manner on the computer. See Figures 68, 69, and 70.

In Figure 68, the relevant program lines are:

```
14   R = 50 : S = 50 : N = -7/5
15   FOR B = 0 TO .2 STEP .1
20   FOR A = 0 TO 10*π STEP .025
30   X = R*COS(A + B) + S*COS(N*A) + 100
40   Y = R*SIN(A + B) + S*SIN(N*A) + 100
70   NEXT B
```

In Figure 69, the relevant program lines are:

```
14   R = 60 : S = 30 : N = 10/3
15   FOR B = 0 TO .3 STEP .1
20   FOR A = 0 TO 6*π STEP .025
30   X = R*COS(A + B) + S*COS(N*A) + 100
40   Y = R*SIN(A+B) + S*SIN(N*A) + 100
70   NEXT B
```

Figure 70 displays a tartan effect which was popular in Victorian times. The relevant program lines are:

```
14   R = 48 : S = 42 : N = 11/2
15   FOR B = 0 TO .3 STEP .1
20   FOR A = 0 TO 4*π STEP .05
30   X = R*COS(A+B) + S*COS(N*A) + 100
40   Y = R*SIN(A+B) + S*SIN(N*A) + 100
70   NEXT B
```

FIGURE 68

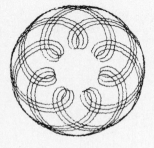

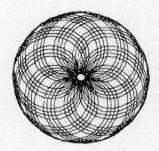

FIGURE 69   **FIGURE 70**

ROTATION AND EXPANSION OF PATTERNS

In Figures 71 and 72 you can see that the combined effect of rotation and expansion can be achieved by linking the rotation element in lines 30 and 40, with increases in R, pattern size. Note that rotation in Figure 71 is slightly slower than in Figure 72, in that rotation proceeds at .1*π for each expansion in Figure 71 and .15*π for each expansion in Figure 72.

   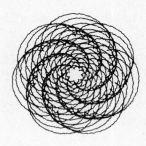

FIGURE 71   **FIGURE 72**

In Figure 71, the relevant program lines are:

```
14   S = 11 : N = 7
15   FOR R = 17 TO 77 STEP 10
20   FOR A = 0 TO 2*π STEP .025
```

30   $X = R*COS(A + \frac{R-20}{100}) + S*COS(N*A) + 100$

40   $Y = R*SIN(A + \frac{R-20}{100}) + S*SIN(N*A) + 100$

```
70   NEXT R
```

In Figure 72, the relevant program lines are:

```
14   N = 9/2
15   FOR R = 20.25 TO 47.25 STEP 4.5
16   S = 2/9*R
20   FOR A = 0 TO 4*π STEP .025
```

30   $X = R*COS(A + \frac{R-20.25}{30}) + S*COS(N*A) + 100$

40   $Y = R*SIN(A + \frac{R-20.25}{30}) + S*SIN(N*A) + 100$

```
70   NEXT R
```

You will note that Figure 71 is identical to Figure 63, only rotated. In Figure 72, line 16 maintains the relationship $S = R/N$, such that with each successive (rotated) expansion, the loops of the pattern remain cusped.

Two other interesting examples of rotation and expansion, illustrating the preceding principles, are shown in Figures 73 and 74.

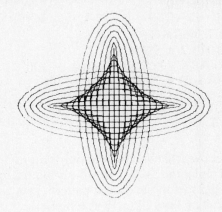

FIGURE 73

In Figure 73, the relevant program lines are:

```
14   R = 25 : N = -1
15   FOR S = 5 TO 60 STEP 5
20   FOR A = 0 TO 2*π STEP .05
30   X = R*COS(A) + S*COS(N*A) + 100
40   Y = R*SIN(A) + S*SIN(N*A) + 100
50   PLOT X,Y
60   NEXT A
70   NEXT S

80   FOR S = 5 TO 60 STEP 5
90   FOR A = 0 TO 2*π STEP .05
100  X = R*COS(A-π) + S*COS(N*A) + 100
110  Y = R*SIN(A-π) + S*SIN(N*A) + 100
120  PLOT X,Y
130  NEXT A
140  NEXT S
```

Lines 14 to 70 are for the horizontal pattern. Lines 80 to 140 are for the vertical pattern.

This program can be improved upon to reduce the number of program lines, as follows:

```
14   R = 25 : N = -1
15   FOR S = 0 TO 65 STEP 5
16   IF S < 65 THEN 20
17   Z = π
18   FOR S = 0 TO 60 STEP 5
20   FOR A = 0 TO 2*π STEP .05
30   X = R*COS(A+Z) + S*COS(N*A) + 100
40   Y = R*SIN(A+Z) + S*SIN(N*A) + 100
50   PLOT X,Y
60   NEXT A
70   NEXT S
```

In fact you will discover that line 18 need only start at S = 5. When S = 0, the computer will replot the circle it previously plotted for S = 0 in line 15.

If you are interested in the central pattern, you can reproduce this (enlarged) by amending lines 14 to 18 as follows:

```
14   R = 45 : N = -1
15   FOR S = 0 TO 50 STEP 5
16   IF S < 50 THEN 20
17   Z = π
18   FOR S = 5 TO 45 STEP 5
```

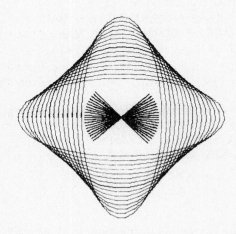

FIGURE 74

The relevant program lines for Figure 74 are:

```
14   S = 64 : N = -1
15   FOR R = 0 TO 32 STEP 4
20   FOR A = 0 TO 2*π STEP .025
30   X = R*COS(A) + S*COS(N*A) + 100
40   Y = R*SIN(A) + S*SIN(N*A) + 100
50   PLOT X,Y
60   NEXT A
70   NEXT R
80   FOR R = 4 TO 32 STEP 4
90   FOR A = 0 TO 2*π STEP .025
100  X = R*COS(A–π) + S*COS(N*A) + 100
110  Y = R*SIN(A–π) + S*SIN(N*A) + 100
120  PLOT X,Y
130  NEXT A
140  NEXT R
```

This program can be improved upon by using an IF . . . THEN statement as with the program for Figure 73.

You will note that line 80 need only start at R = 4. When R = 0, the computer will replot the circle it previously plotted in line 15.

STRAIGHT LINE

The epicyclic motion of the Geometric Pen or Lathe can also produce straight lines. It will be recalled from Chapters 5 and 6 that where R = S, the loops of an epicyclical pattern meet at the center. In the special case where N = -1, the loops merge into a straight line. This enables us to generate several interesting patterns based on the principle of rotation.

The program lines to generate the central pattern in Figure 74 are:

```
150  R = 15 : S = 15 : N = -1
160  FOR Z = 3*π/2 TO 5*π/2 STEP π/10
170  FOR A = 0 TO 2*π STEP .075
180  X = R*COS(A+Z) + S*COS(N*A) + 100
190  Y = R*SIN(A+Z) + S*SIN(N*A) + 100
200  PLOT X,Y
210  NEXT A
220  NEXT Z
```

You will note that if line 160 were changed to:

160   FOR Z = 0 TO 2*π STEP π/10

the computer would plot 20 lines equally spaced in a circular pattern.

The long-winded program used here was done so for illustrative purposes. You may be able to improve on it to reduce the number of program lines.

One further pattern based on the concept of rotation is Figure 75. This pattern involves several program loops:

- Lines 13 - 80, to produce variable line length
- Lines 15 - 70, to produce rotation of lines
- Lines 20 - 60, to draw lines.

The relevant program lines are:

```
13   FOR G = –π/6 TO π/6 STEP π/24
14   R = 50 – 40*ABS(G): S = 50 – 40*ABS(G): N = –1
15   FOR Z = 0 TO 2*π STEP π/3
20   FOR A = 0 TO 2*π STEP .075
30   X = R*COS(A+Z+G) + S*COS(N*A) + 100
40   Y = R*SIN(A+Z+G) + S*SIN(N*A) + 100
50   PLOT X,Y
60   NEXT A
70   NEXT Z
80   NEXT G
```

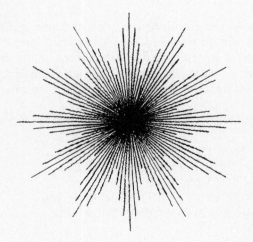

FIGURE 75

HORIZONTAL MOVEMENT OF A PATTERN

Let us also consider movement in a straight line, as shown in Figure 76. The relevant program lines are:

```
14   R = 20 : S = 20 : N = 3
15   FOR B = 0 TO 40 STEP 10
20   FOR A = 0 TO 2*π STEP .05
30   X = R*COS(A) + S*COS(N*A) + 80 + B
40   Y = R*SIN(A) + S*SIN(N*A) + 100
50   PLOT X,Y
60   NEXT A
70   NEXT B
```

This program will generate movement in a horizontal direction. By inserting B in line 40 instead of line 30, the program will generate movement in a vertical direction (which, of course would produce an entirely different pattern).

Alternatively, inserting B in lines 30 and 40 will produce movement in an angular direction. Of course, the sign (positive or negative) of B determines whether the pattern will move from left to right or vice versa when plotted by the computer.

These are all straight line movements. However, you may care to experiment with others. For example, Figures 80 and 81 illustrate the effect of a pattern moving in an epicyclic path.

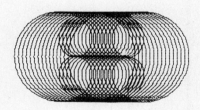

FIGURE 76

PATTERN PROBLEMS

If you have reached this stage, perhaps you would like a few problems to ponder over.

Figure 77 is an example of successive expansion. However, you will have to employ the principles of rotation to avoid plotting it sideways on the computer screen.

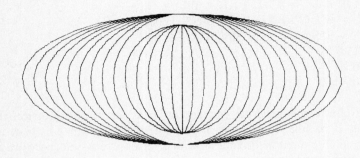

FIGURE 77

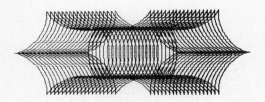

FIGURE 78

Figure 78 is a development of Figure 29. It involves right and left horizontal movement as well as rotation. Note the illusion of circles created by successive overlapping.

Figure 79 is a development of Figure 24, although the coefficients have been changed slightly, to R = 46 and S = 34. This pattern involves both horizontal and vertical movements.

FIGURE 79

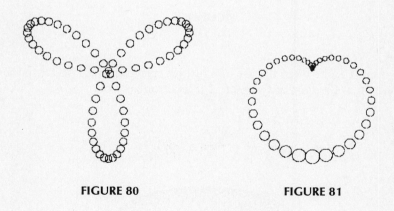

FIGURE 80   **FIGURE 81**

Figure 80 is also a development of Figure 24. Here the pattern is a circle moving in an epicyclic path, rather than in a straight line as previously.

Figure 81 involves a similar program to Figure 80, except that the circles increase and decrease in size.

Figure 82 involves changing the coefficients R and S with each expansion and vertical movement. Note that it is necessary to maintain the relationship S = R/N, in order that successive patterns are cusped. This pattern often appears in nineteenth century literature coupled with its reflection, giving the appearance of an open clam shell. Can you reproduce this?

FIGURE 82

Figure 83 involves the use of a further epicyclic wheel. Refer to the discussion at the start of Chapter 11 if this troubles you.

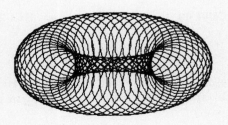

FIGURE 83

8 Plotting Compound Epicyclic Patterns

The patterns illustrated to this stage have all been generated by simulating the Geometric Pen or Geometric Lathe in the "simple" mode. If you add a further epicyclic wheel, the "compound" mode of the pen or lathe will produce an entirely different range of patterns. In referring to the compound attachment to the lathe, Bazley said:

> The interesting character of the curves produced is so much greater, that the amateur who has such an apparatus at his disposal will not often wish to reduce its capabilities to the simple form.

The fact that this is so will be readily apparent from the rich variety of patterns that follow.

Referring to earlier chapters, you will recall the equations necessary to generate a circle:

$$X = R*COS(A)$$
$$Y = R*SIN(A)$$

where a numerical value is substituted for the coefficient R. In fact, the value of R is equal to the radius of the circle.

It will also be recalled that the equations necessary to generate simple epicyclic curves or patterns are:

$$X = R*COS(A) + S*COS(N*A)$$
$$Y = R*SIN(A) + S*SIN(N*A)$$

where numerical values are substituted for the coefficients R, S, and N. Here the sum of (R + S) is equal to the radius of the curve.

From this you may deduce that the equations necessary to generate compound epicyclic curves or patterns are:

$$X = R*COS(A) + S*COS(N*A) + T*COS(M*A)$$
$$Y = R*SIN(A) + S*SIN(N*A) + T*SIN(M*A)$$

where numerical values are substituted for the coefficients R, S, T, N, and M. Here the sum of (R + S + T) is equal to the radius of the curve.

The centering of such curves on the computer screen is achieved in the same way as with circles and simple epicyclic curves.

Similarly, the program necessary to generate compound epicyclic curves is exactly the same as for other curves, except that the step size in line 20 has been reduced:

```
10   HCOLOR
15   R =  : S =  : T =
16   N = : M =
20   FOR A = 0 TO 2*π STEP .01
30   X = R*COS(A) + S*COS(N*A) + T*COS(M*A) + 100
40   Y = R*SIN(A) + S*SIN(N*A) + T*SIN(M*A) + 100
50   PLOT X,Y
60   NEXT A
```

Let us now type this program into the computer with the following information for lines 15 and 16:

```
15   R = 30 : S = 30 : T = -8
16   N = -3 : M = 9
```

On running the program, the computer will produce the pattern shown in Figure 84.

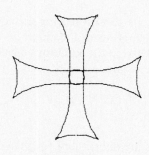

FIGURE 84

PLOTTING PATTERNS FROM THE TABLES

You may plot any of the compound epicyclic patterns in this book from the Appendix tables by merely keying in values for R, S, T, N, and M as lines 15 and 16 in the general program. Pattern size, program length, and step size may need to be varied according to the principles outlined below.

To make a pattern larger or smaller to fit the computer screen, R, S, and T must all be increased or decreased in proportion.

For example, if:

R = 20 : S = 30 : T = 40

then the following coefficients would produce progressively larger patterns:

R = 30 : S = 45 : T = 60
R = 40 : S = 60 : T = 80
R = 50 : S = 75 : T = 100

For some patterns, such as Figure 593, it is possible to enlarge the pattern more after repositioning it on the screen. This can be achieved by changing the constants 100 and 100 in lines 30 and 40 of the general program set out earlier in this chapter.

It will be recalled from earlier chapters that the length of a program (that is, line 20) necessary to generate a circle is $2*\pi$ (N not being used in the parametric equations required to generate a circle). The length necessary to generate a simple epicyclic curve is $2*\pi$ where N is an integer and $2*B*\pi$ where N is a fraction (A/B) reduced to its lowest form (B being the denominator of the fraction).

The principle established for a simple epicyclic curve above applies equally to compound epicyclic curves. Accordingly, if you wish to plot a pattern from the following coefficients:

R = 10 : S = 50 : T = -13
N = -7/3 : M = -47/3

it would be necessary to amend line 20 as follows:

20   FOR A = 0 TO 6*π STEP .01

As with other curves, dots on the computer screen can be made closer together or farther apart by altering the step size in line 20. For example, the following adjustments would produce progressively closer dots:

```
20   FOR A = 0 TO 2*π STEP .1
20   FOR A = 0 TO 2*π STEP .05
20   FOR A = 0 TO 2*π STEP .01
```

Instead of having to key in line 20 each time the length of the program or step size needs changing, you may prefer to key in the following:

```
18   B =
19   C =
20   FOR A = 0 TO B*π STEP C
```

By introducing B and C, line 18 or 19 can be retyped where necessary rather than the long-winded line 20; similarly if the computer keyboard does not have the symbol π.

INTERPRETATION OF COMPOUND EPICYCLIC PATTERNS

The mathematics of simple epicyclic patterns were worked out as early as 1843 by Augustus de Morgan, Professor of Mathematics, University College, London, and published in the *Penny Cyclopaedia*. The mathematics of compound epicyclic curves were never worked out. In 1873, Savory wrote:

> The scientific knowledge required to understand the [compound Geometric Lathe] would be so great that I doubt if there is a person existing who could describe the course of a line that would be produced . . . it is quite certain that if we have to wait for a scientific knowledge of the [compound Geometric Lathe] before we can commence using it, we shall have to wait a very long time.

Savory's remarks were an observation rather than a criticism of Victorian mathematicians. The truth is that compound epicyclic patterns were such an esoteric area of mathematics that little interest was shown by professional mathematicians.

Understandably this neglect by mathematicians has persisted. We are not aware of any recent authority on the subject and offer the following interpretation of compound patterns only as guidelines rather than as conclusive or exhaustic rules.

1. Interpretation of compound epicyclic patterns is as for simple consecutive and circulating epicyclic patterns (that is, irrespective of whether N and M are integral or fractional):

- Where N is positive, the loops are internal.
- Where N is negative, the loops are external.
- Where N is positive, the number of loops is equal to the numerator minus the denominator.
- Where N is negative, the number of loops is equal to the numerator plus the denominator.

2. With simple epicyclic patterns, it was possible to lay down rules determining the frequency and shape of loops comprising a pattern. As discussed in Chapters 5 and 6, frequency was dependent upon the numerical value of N, and shape was dependent upon the relationship between R and S.

With compound epicyclic patterns, frequency is again dependent upon the numerical value of N, as discussed above. The shape of loops, however, is not so easily determined. The term "loops" is used here in the broadest sense. "Compartments" would perhaps be a better word.

Such compartments or segments are often of an unsymmetrical or unattractive nature, but when overlapped, they produce a pattern of symmetrical and pleasing appearance. Accordingly, the shape of each compartment is not of great significance, the general appearance of a pattern being dependent more upon the successive overlapping of compartments than upon their individual shape.

This is particularly so, the larger the numerical value of N. Take Figure 594, for example. Here the triangular compartments are lost as successive overlapping creates a different overall appearance.

For small values of N, it will be seen that circulating patterns (that is, where N is fractional) generally have a more striking appearance than consecutive patterns (that is, where N is integral). This property was also evident with simple epicyclic patterns.

3. Where compartments are reasonably confined and overlapping is minimal, you may care to ascertain the relationship between the coefficients. For example, take the star patterns in Figures 136, 141, and 152:

Figure	Points	R	S	T	N	M
136	4	30	30	11	–3	5
141	6	30	30	15	–5	7
152	9	30	30	18	–8	10

By either interpolation or extrapolation, you will readily be able to ascertain the respective value of R, S, T, N, and M required to generate star patterns with different numbers of points. However, you will note that T should not be increased at the same rate as N and M. For example, for star patterns of 15 and 20 points respectively, the coefficients are (approximately):

Points	R	S	T	N	M
15	30	30	21	-14	16
20	30	30	23	-19	21

4. Problems arise, however, where compartments are not so reasonably confined. In this case overlapping quickly occurs and the general appearance of the pattern changes. For example, take the cross patterns in Figures 252 and 257:

Figure	Points	R	S	T	N	M
252	4	30	30	-8	-3	9
257	6	30	30	-9	-5	13

Again, by interpolation or extrapolation, you will be able to ascertain the respective values of R, S, T, N, and M required to generate cross patterns with different numbers of points. However, you will note that if you choose a numerical value of N greater than – 6 (that is, with more than seven points), the compartments will overlap and the pattern will take on an altogether different appearance, of which Figure 273 is an example.

5. From the above it is apparent that N is the dominant coefficient in determining the shape of a compound epicyclic pattern, in that it determines the number of loops or compartments. Where N is large however, there appears to be a relationship between N and M which determines the number of major compartments (while N will still determine the number of loops or minor compartments). Compare the following values for Figures 589, 590, 591, and 592:

Figure	Major Compartments	N	M	N – M
589	2	57	-53	4
590	3	55	-50	5
591	4	55	-49	6
592	9	61	-50	11

It is apparent that the number of major compartments of these patterns is equal to the difference between N and M minus 2. Again by interpolation or extrapolation, you will be able to ascertain coefficients of N and M required to generate similar patterns with different numbers of major compartments.

6. Some patterns (such as Figures 593 to 597) will be plotted sideways on the computer screen. They can be uprighted by transposing lines 30, 40, and 50 of the general program at the start of this chapter:

```
30  X = R*SIN(A) + S*SIN(N*A) + T*SIN(M*A) + 100
40  Y = R*COS(A) + S*COS(N*A) + T*COS(M*A) + 100
50  PLOT X, 200 — Y
```

7. With simple epicyclic curves, it was possible to generate the same curve with two different sets of coefficients (refer to Chapters 5 and 6). With compound epicyclic curves, it is possible to generate the same curve with four different sets of coefficients. The following table will assist those interested to determine equivalent sets of coefficients:

	N	M	R	S	T
(a)	N	M	R	S	T
	1/N	M/N	S	R	T
	M	N	R	T	S
	M/N	1/N	S	T	R
(b)	−N	−M	R	S	T
	−1/N	M/N	S	R	T
	−M	−N	R	T	S
	M/N	−1/N	S	T	R
(c)	N	−M	R	S	T
	1/N	−M/N	S	R	T
	−M	N	R	T	S
	−M/N	1/N	S	T	R
(d)	−N	M	R	S	T
	−1/N	−M/N	S	R	T
	M	−N	R	T	S
	−M/N	−1/N	S	T	R

By way of explanation, Figure 121 fits into group (a) above, both N and M being positive. It will be seen that the same pattern can be generated from any of the following four sets of coefficients:

N	M	R	S	T
13/5	21/5	40	20	8
5/13	21/13	20	40	8
21/5	13/5	40	8	20
21/13	5/13	20	8	40

Figure 244 fits into group (b) above, both N and M being negative. Accordingly, the same pattern can be generated from any of the following four sets of coefficients:

N	M	R	S	T
–7/3	–9	40	20	11
–3/7	27/7	20	40	11
–9	–7/3	40	11	20
27/7	–3/7	20	11	40

Figure 540 fits into group (c) above, N being positive and M negative. The same pattern can be generated from any of the following four sets of coefficients:

N	M	R	S	T
9/2	–33/2	40	20	–4
2/9	–11/3	20	40	–4
–33/2	9/2	40	–4	20
–11/3	2/9	20	–4	40

Figure 278 fits into group (d) above, N being negative and M positive. The same pattern can be generated from any of the following four sets of coefficients:

N	M	R	S	T
–8	19	20	40	10
–1/8	–19/8	40	20	10
19	–8	20	10	40
–19/8	–1/8	40	10	20

It seems that this information was of interest to users of the Geometric Lathe, as it would have assisted in the choice of change-wheels. It is largely of academic interest to users of the computer. As in Chapter 5, this is presented here to eliminate any confusion readers may have in generating exactly the same pattern with different sets of coefficients.

COMPOUND PATTERNS

Patterns on pages 70 to 160 can be reproduced by substituting the coefficients given in the Appendix into this general program:

```
10   HCOLOR
15   R =  : S =  : T =
16   N =  : M =
20   FOR A = 0 TO 2*π STEP .01
30   X = R*COS(A) + S*COS(N*A) + T*COS(M*A) + 100
40   Y = R*SIN(A) + S*SIN(N*A) + T*SIN(M*A) + 100
50   PLOT X,Y
60   NEXT A
```

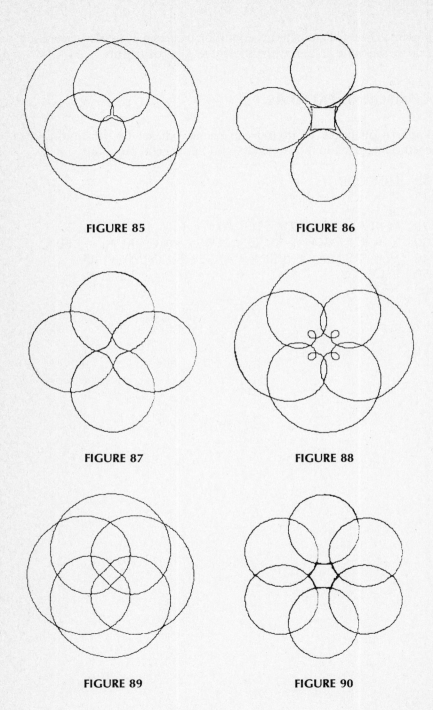

FIGURE 85

FIGURE 86

FIGURE 87

FIGURE 88

FIGURE 89

FIGURE 90

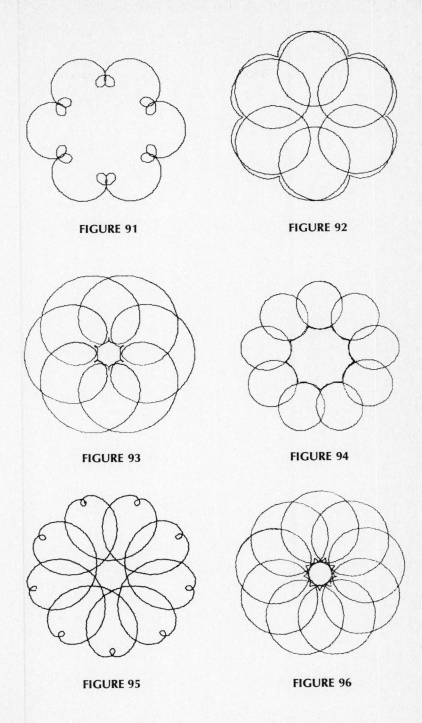

FIGURE 91

FIGURE 92

FIGURE 93

FIGURE 94

FIGURE 95

FIGURE 96

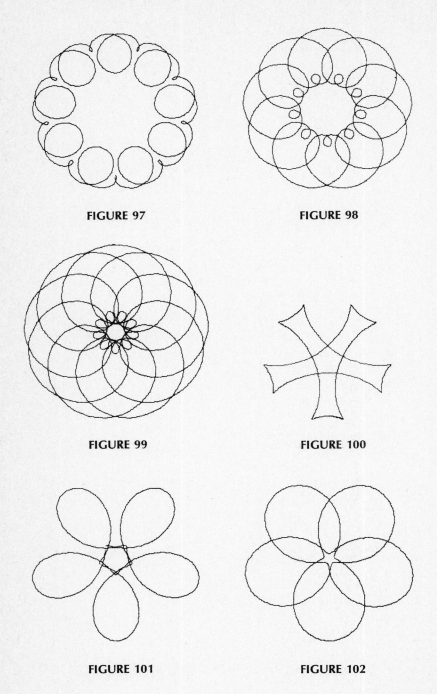

FIGURE 97   **FIGURE 98**

FIGURE 99   **FIGURE 100**

FIGURE 101   **FIGURE 102**

FIGURE 103

FIGURE 104

FIGURE 105

FIGURE 106

FIGURE 107

FIGURE 108

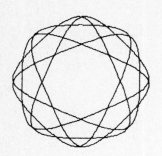

FIGURE 109

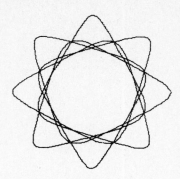

FIGURE 110

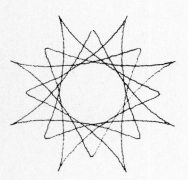

FIGURE 111

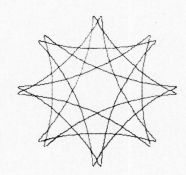

FIGURE 112

FIGURE 113

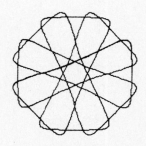

FIGURE 114

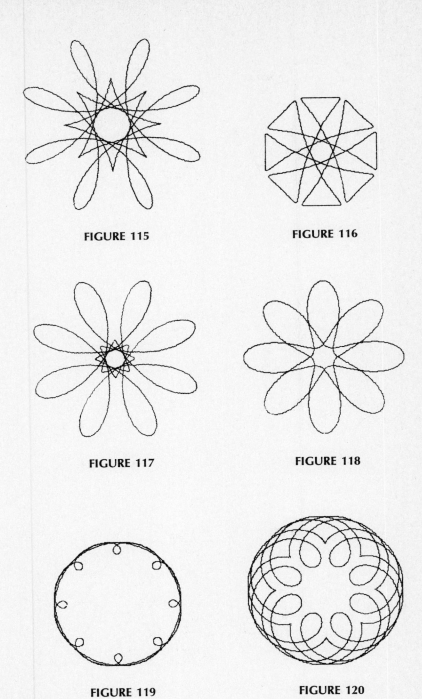

FIGURE 115

FIGURE 116

FIGURE 117

FIGURE 118

FIGURE 119

FIGURE 120

FIGURE 121

FIGURE 122

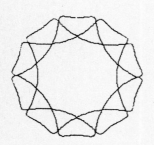

FIGURE 123

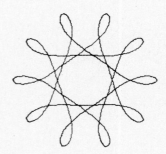

FIGURE 124

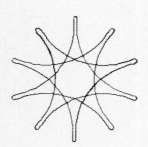

FIGURE 125

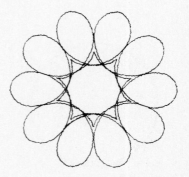

FIGURE 126

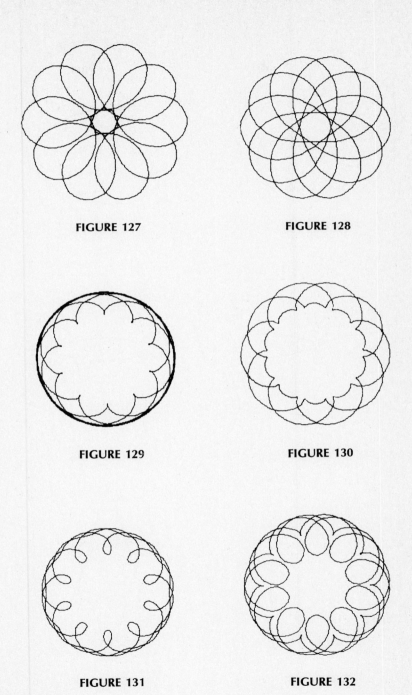

FIGURE 127

FIGURE 128

FIGURE 129

FIGURE 130

FIGURE 131

FIGURE 132

FIGURE 133

FIGURE 134

FIGURE 135

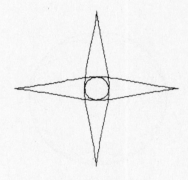

FIGURE 136

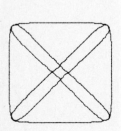

FIGURE 137

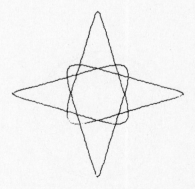

FIGURE 138

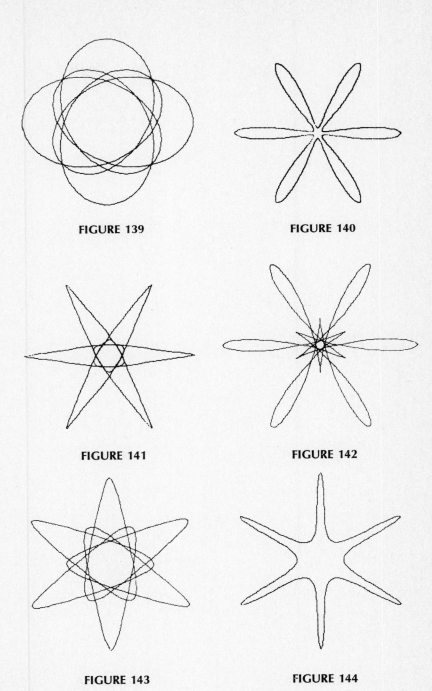

FIGURE 139

FIGURE 140

FIGURE 141

FIGURE 142

FIGURE 143

FIGURE 144

FIGURE 145

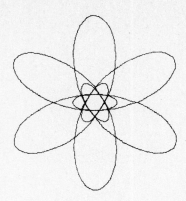

FIGURE 146

FIGURE 147

FIGURE 148

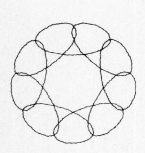

FIGURE 149

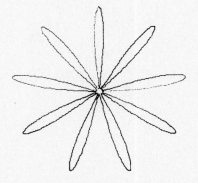

FIGURE 150

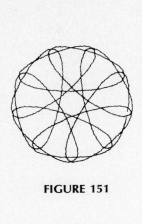

FIGURE 151

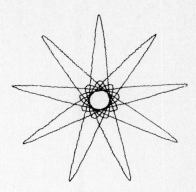

FIGURE 152

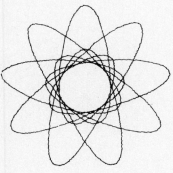

FIGURE 153

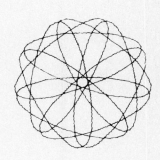

FIGURE 154

FIGURE 155

FIGURE 156

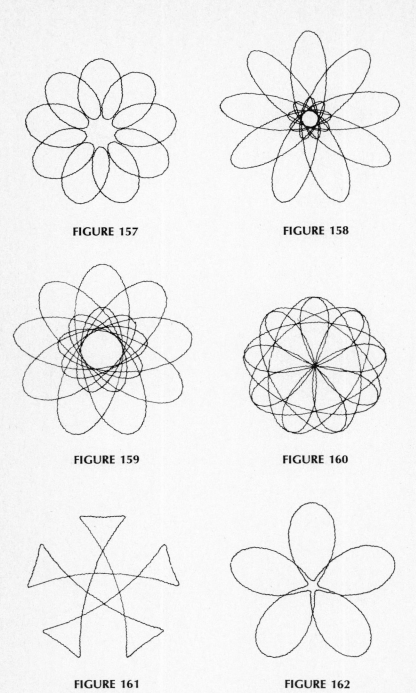

FIGURE 157

FIGURE 158

FIGURE 159

FIGURE 160

FIGURE 161

FIGURE 162

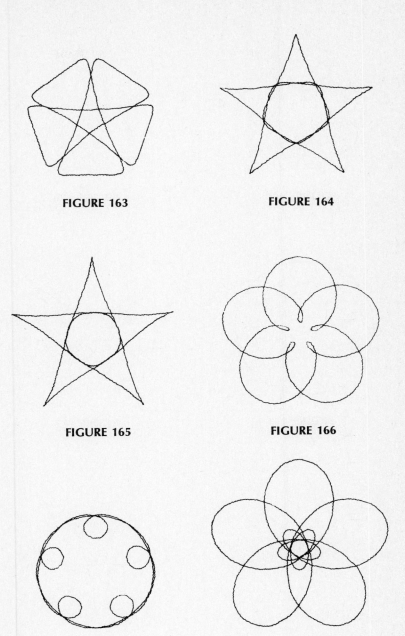

FIGURE 163

FIGURE 164

FIGURE 165

FIGURE 166

FIGURE 167

FIGURE 168

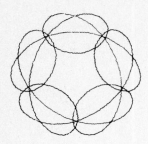

FIGURE 169

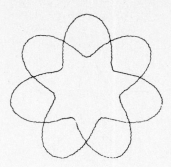

FIGURE 170

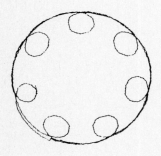

FIGURE 171

FIGURE 172

FIGURE 173

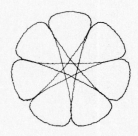

FIGURE 174

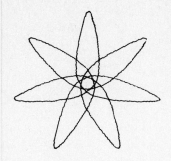

FIGURE 175

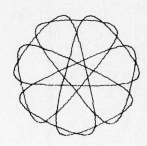

FIGURE 176

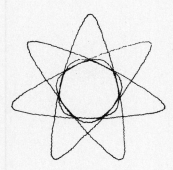

FIGURE 177

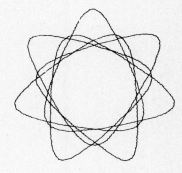

FIGURE 178

FIGURE 179

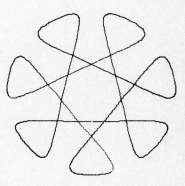

FIGURE 180

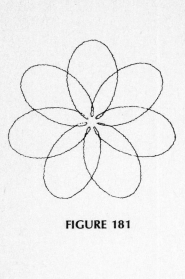

FIGURE 181

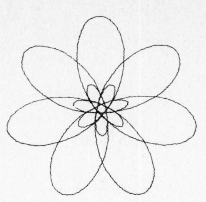

FIGURE 182

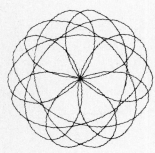

FIGURE 183

FIGURE 184

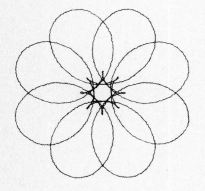

FIGURE 185

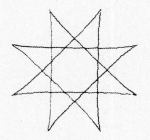

FIGURE 186

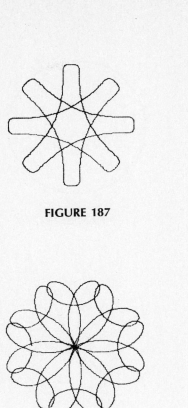

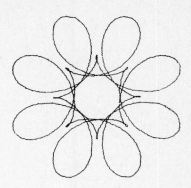

FIGURE 187

FIGURE 188

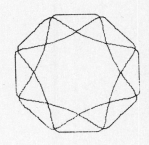

FIGURE 189

FIGURE 190

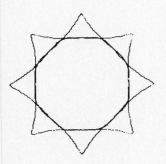

FIGURE 191

FIGURE 192

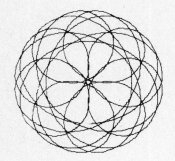

FIGURE 193

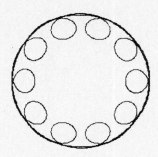

FIGURE 194

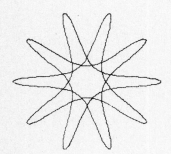

FIGURE 195

FIGURE 196

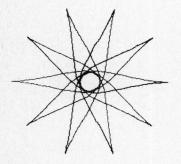

FIGURE 197

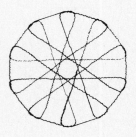

FIGURE 198

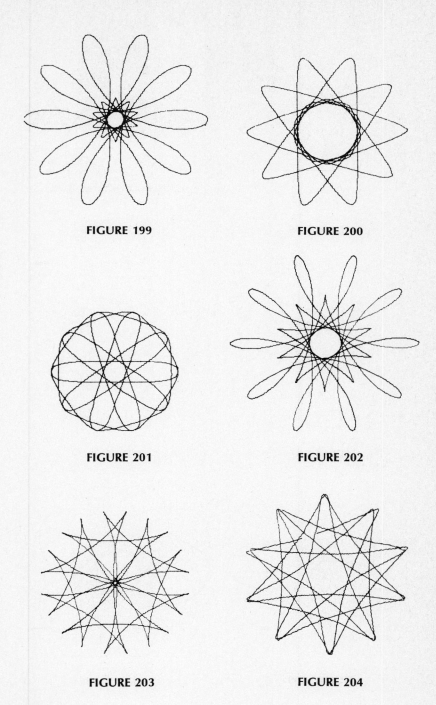

FIGURE 199

FIGURE 200

FIGURE 201

FIGURE 202

FIGURE 203

FIGURE 204

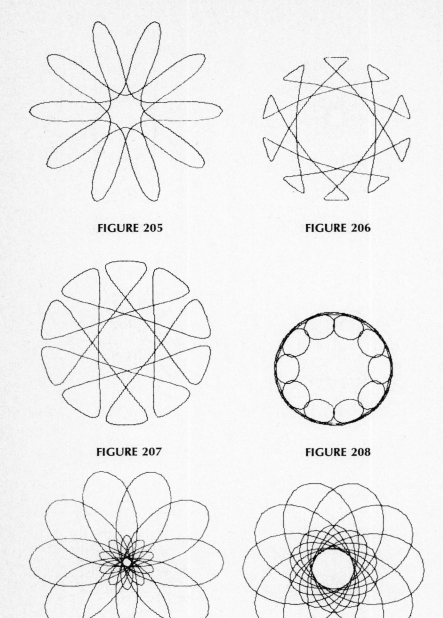

FIGURE 205

FIGURE 206

FIGURE 207

FIGURE 208

FIGURE 209

FIGURE 210

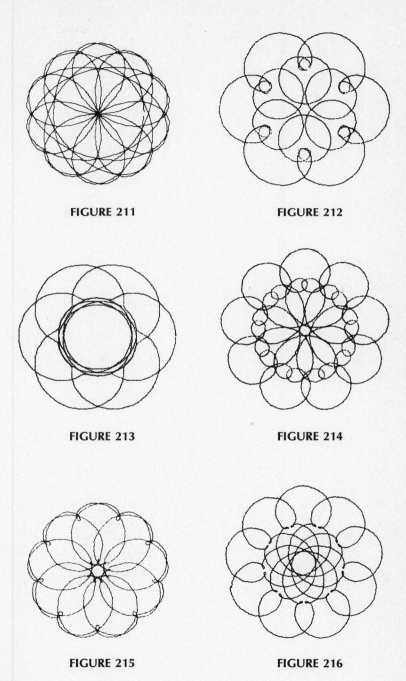

FIGURE 211

FIGURE 212

FIGURE 213

FIGURE 214

FIGURE 215

FIGURE 216

FIGURE 217

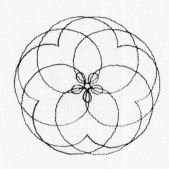

FIGURE 218

FIGURE 219

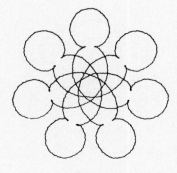

FIGURE 220

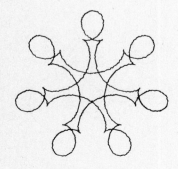

FIGURE 221

FIGURE 222

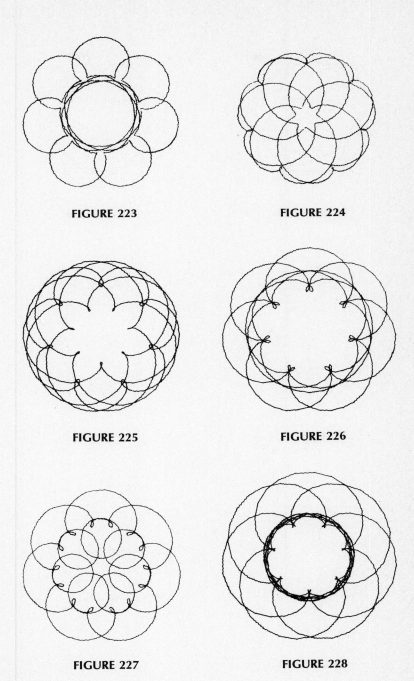

FIGURE 223

FIGURE 224

FIGURE 225

FIGURE 226

FIGURE 227

FIGURE 228

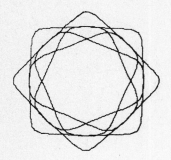

FIGURE 229

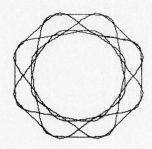

FIGURE 230

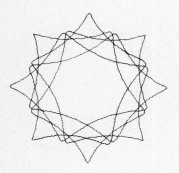

FIGURE 231

FIGURE 232

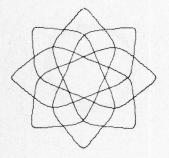

FIGURE 233

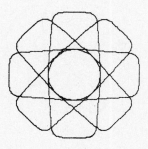

FIGURE 234

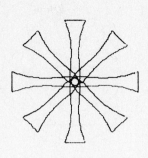

FIGURE 235

FIGURE 236

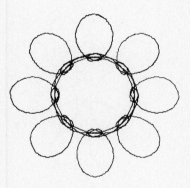

FIGURE 237

FIGURE 238

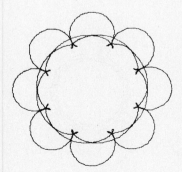

FIGURE 239

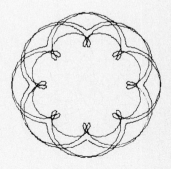

FIGURE 240

FIGURE 241

FIGURE 242

FIGURE 243

FIGURE 244

FIGURE 245

FIGURE 246

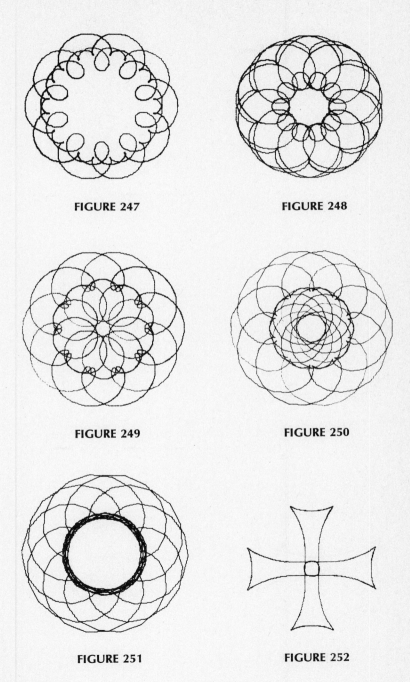

FIGURE 247

FIGURE 248

FIGURE 249

FIGURE 250

FIGURE 251

FIGURE 252

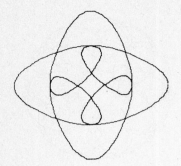

FIGURE 253

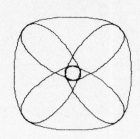

FIGURE 254

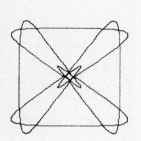

FIGURE 255

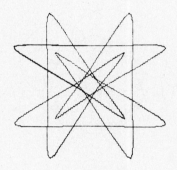

FIGURE 256

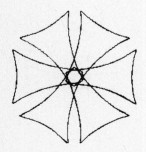

FIGURE 257

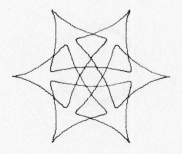

FIGURE 258

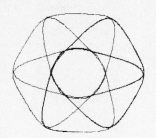

FIGURE 259

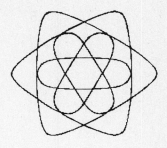

FIGURE 260

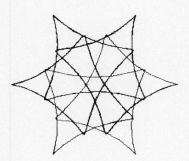

FIGURE 261

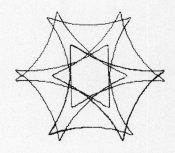

FIGURE 262

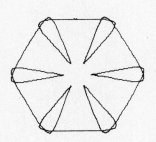

FIGURE 263

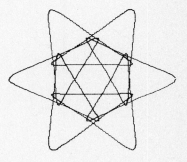

FIGURE 264

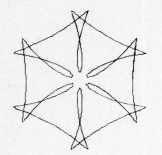

FIGURE 265

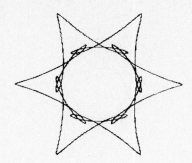

FIGURE 266

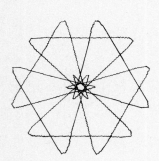

FIGURE 267

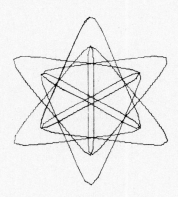

FIGURE 268

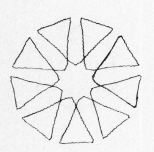

FIGURE 269

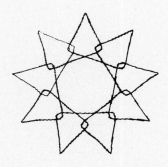

FIGURE 270

FIGURE 271

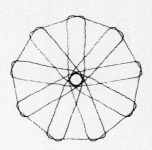

FIGURE 272

FIGURE 273

FIGURE 274

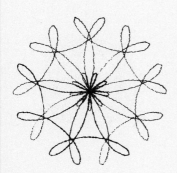

FIGURE 275

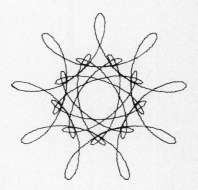

FIGURE 276

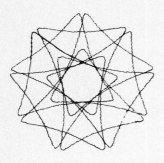

FIGURE 277

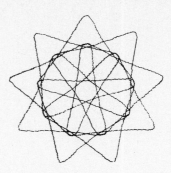

FIGURE 278

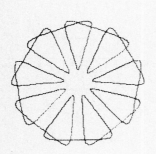

FIGURE 279

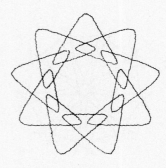

FIGURE 280

FIGURE 281

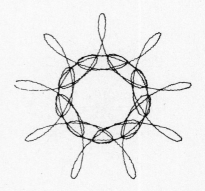

FIGURE 282

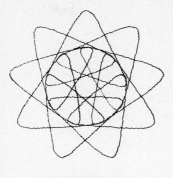

FIGURE 283

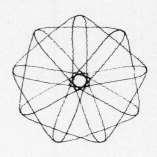

FIGURE 284

FIGURE 285

FIGURE 286

FIGURE 287

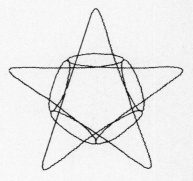

FIGURE 288

FIGURE 289

FIGURE 290

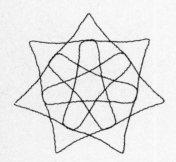

FIGURE 291

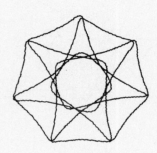

FIGURE 292

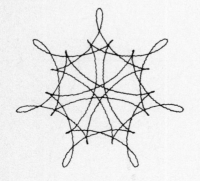

FIGURE 293

FIGURE 294

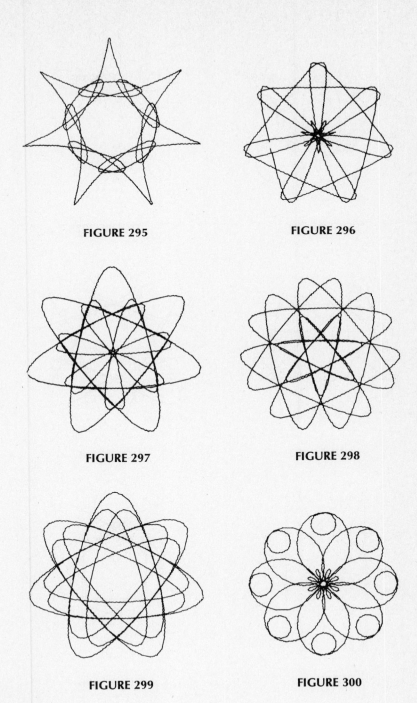

FIGURE 295

FIGURE 296

FIGURE 297

FIGURE 298

FIGURE 299

FIGURE 300

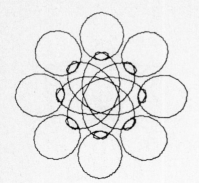

FIGURE 301

FIGURE 302

FIGURE 303

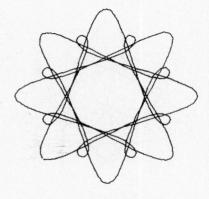

FIGURE 304

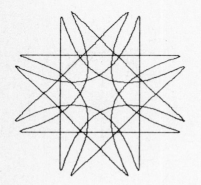

FIGURE 305

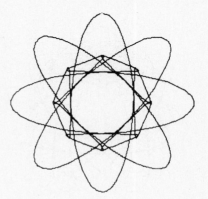

FIGURE 306

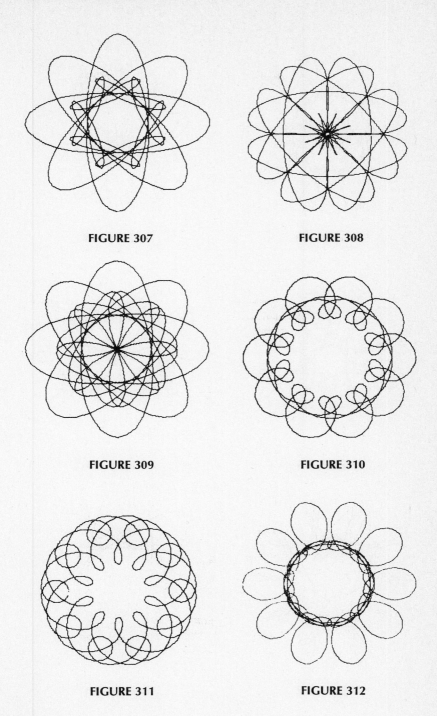

FIGURE 307

FIGURE 308

FIGURE 309

FIGURE 310

FIGURE 311

FIGURE 312

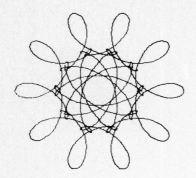

FIGURE 313

FIGURE 314

FIGURE 315

FIGURE 316

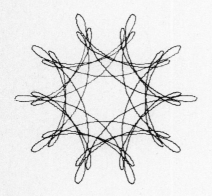

FIGURE 317

FIGURE 318

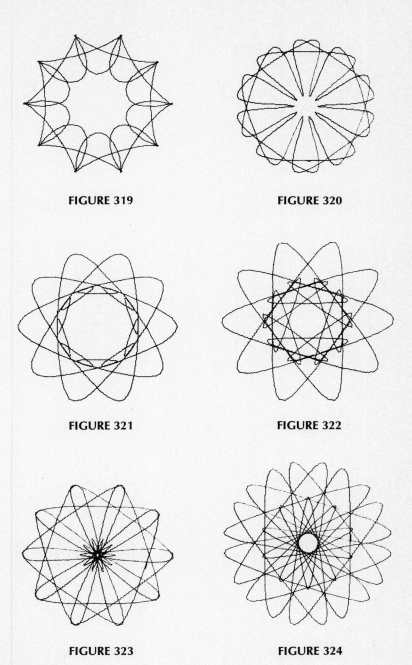

FIGURE 319

FIGURE 320

FIGURE 321

FIGURE 322

FIGURE 323

FIGURE 324

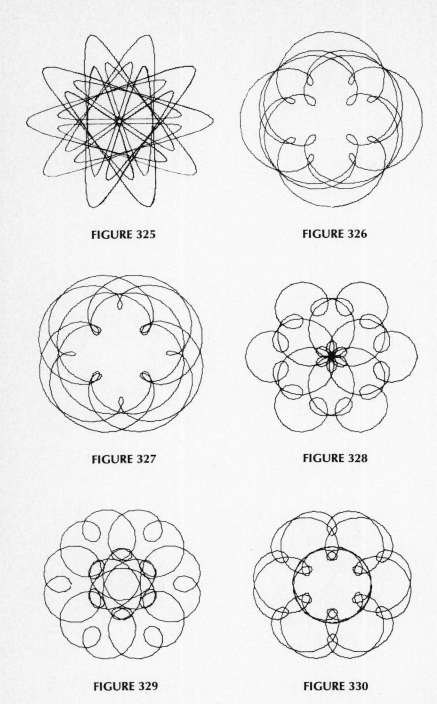

FIGURE 325

FIGURE 326

FIGURE 327

FIGURE 328

FIGURE 329

FIGURE 330

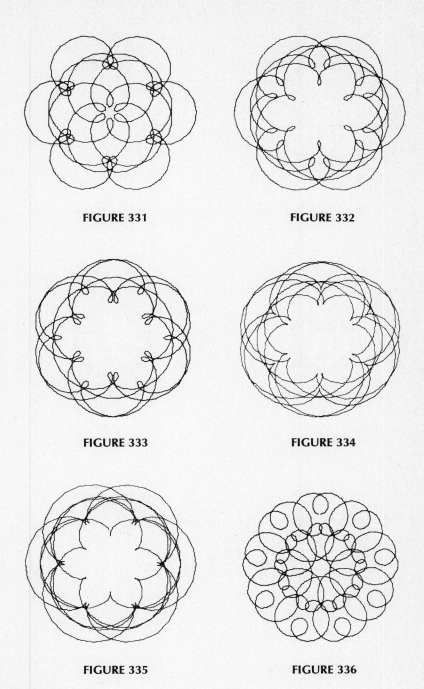

FIGURE 331

FIGURE 332

FIGURE 333

FIGURE 334

FIGURE 335

FIGURE 336

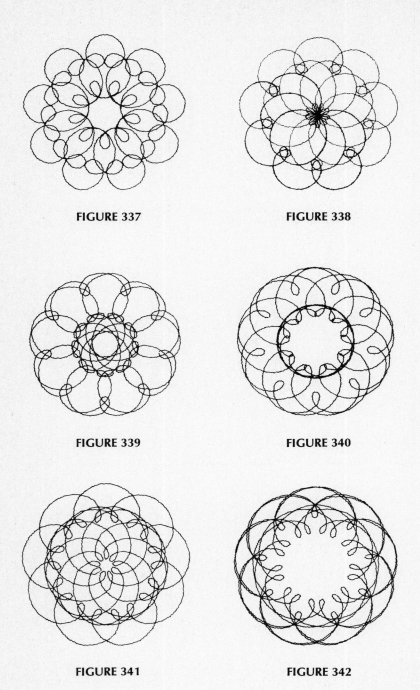

FIGURE 337

FIGURE 338

FIGURE 339

FIGURE 340

FIGURE 341

FIGURE 342

FIGURE 343

FIGURE 344

FIGURE 345

FIGURE 346

FIGURE 347

FIGURE 348

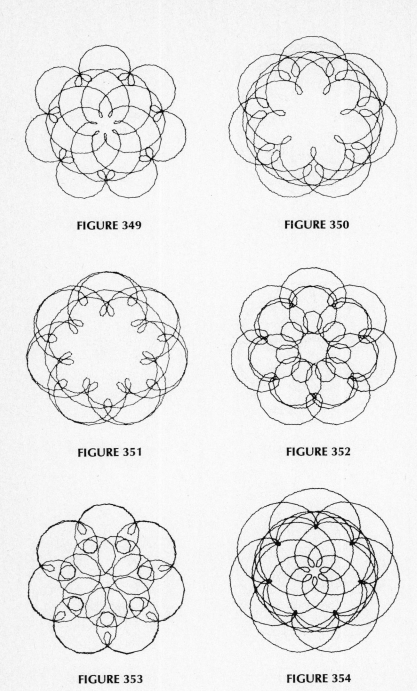

FIGURE 349

FIGURE 350

FIGURE 351

FIGURE 352

FIGURE 353

FIGURE 354

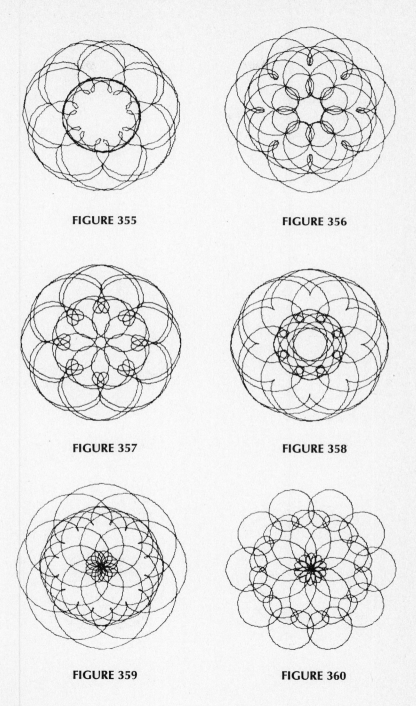

FIGURE 355

FIGURE 356

FIGURE 357

FIGURE 358

FIGURE 359

FIGURE 360

FIGURE 361   **FIGURE 362**

FIGURE 363   **FIGURE 364**

FIGURE 365   **FIGURE 366**

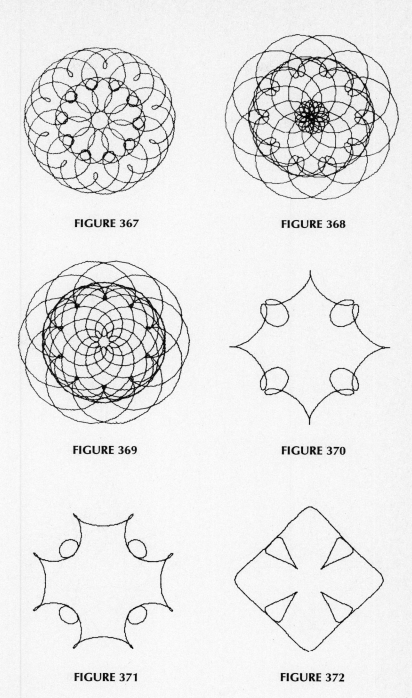

FIGURE 367

FIGURE 368

FIGURE 369

FIGURE 370

FIGURE 371

FIGURE 372

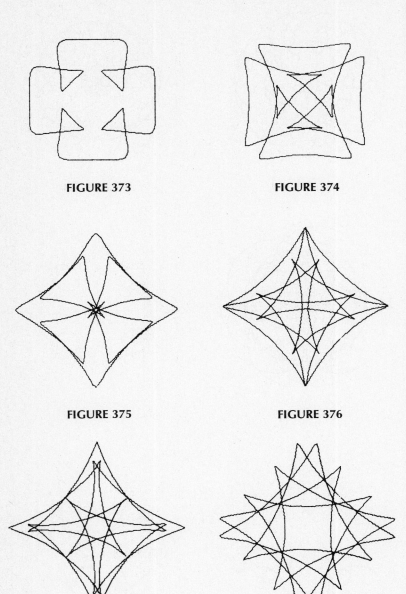

FIGURE 373   **FIGURE 374**

FIGURE 375   **FIGURE 376**

FIGURE 377   **FIGURE 378**

FIGURE 379

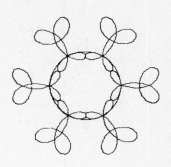

FIGURE 380

FIGURE 381

FIGURE 382

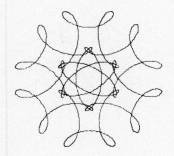

FIGURE 383

FIGURE 384

FIGURE 385

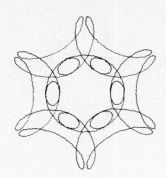

FIGURE 386

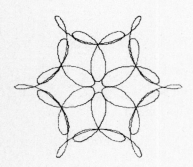

FIGURE 387

FIGURE 388

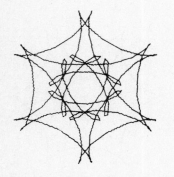

FIGURE 389

FIGURE 390

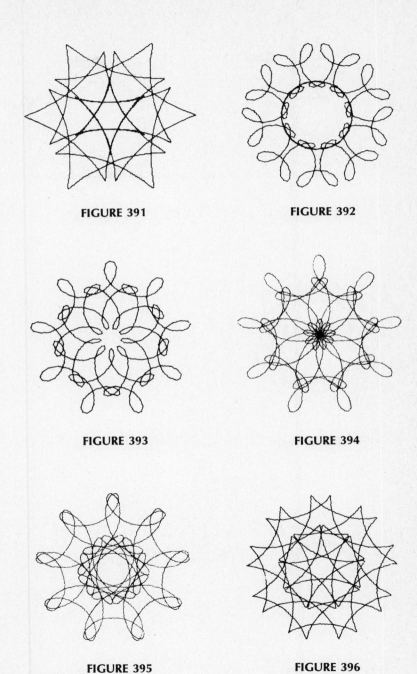

FIGURE 391

FIGURE 392

FIGURE 393

FIGURE 394

FIGURE 395

FIGURE 396

FIGURE 397

FIGURE 398

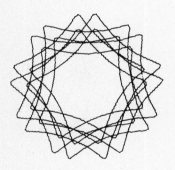

FIGURE 399

FIGURE 400

FIGURE 401

FIGURE 402

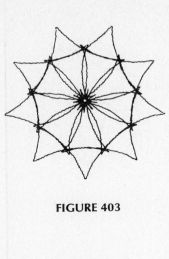

FIGURE 403

FIGURE 404

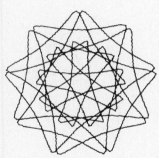

FIGURE 405

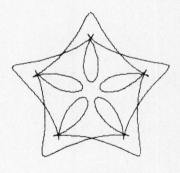

FIGURE 406

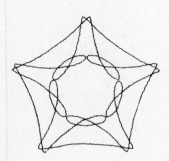

FIGURE 407

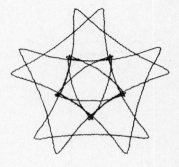

FIGURE 408

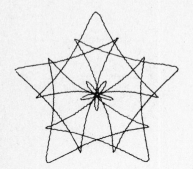

FIGURE 409

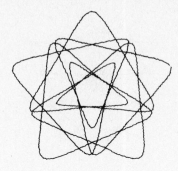

FIGURE 410

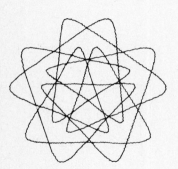

FIGURE 411

FIGURE 412

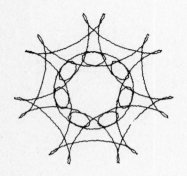

FIGURE 413

FIGURE 414

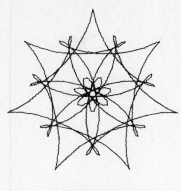

FIGURE 415

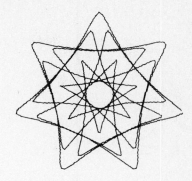

FIGURE 416

FIGURE 417

FIGURE 418

FIGURE 419

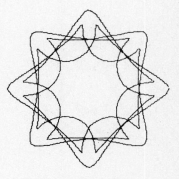

FIGURE 420

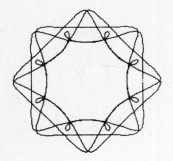

FIGURE 421

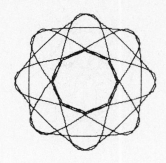

FIGURE 422

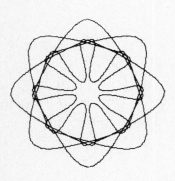

FIGURE 423

FIGURE 424

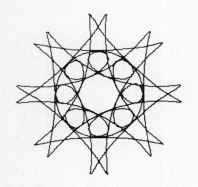

FIGURE 425

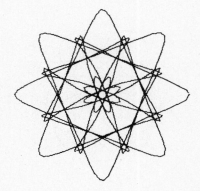

FIGURE 426

FIGURE 427

FIGURE 428

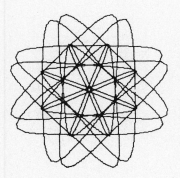

FIGURE 429

FIGURE 430

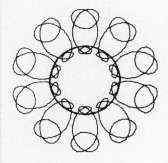

FIGURE 431

FIGURE 432

FIGURE 433

FIGURE 434

FIGURE 435

FIGURE 436

FIGURE 437

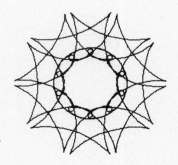

FIGURE 438

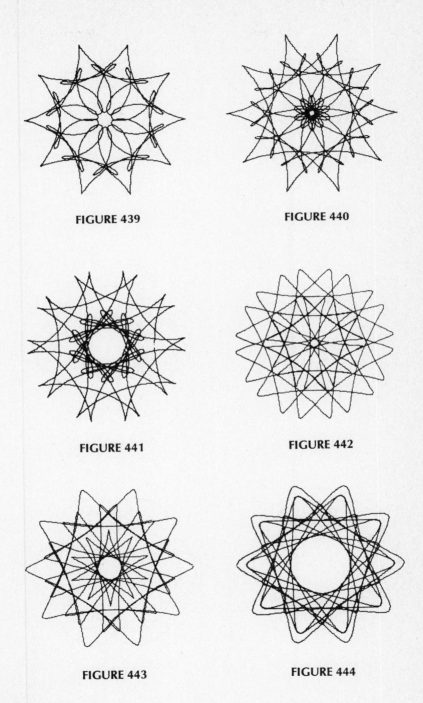

FIGURE 439

FIGURE 440

FIGURE 441

FIGURE 442

FIGURE 443

FIGURE 444

FIGURE 445

FIGURE 446

FIGURE 447

FIGURE 448

FIGURE 449

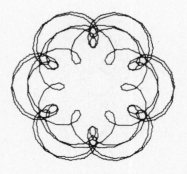

FIGURE 450

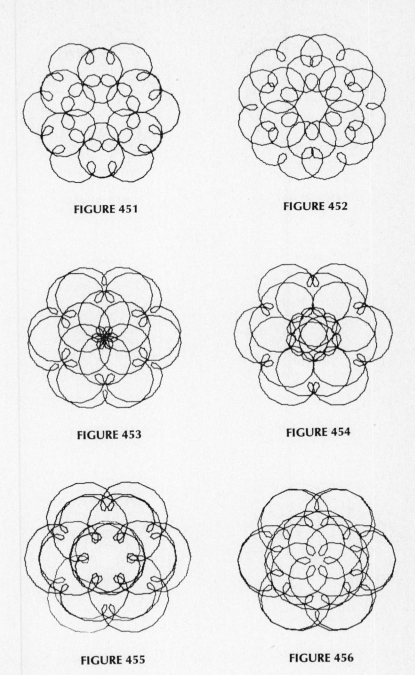

FIGURE 451

FIGURE 452

FIGURE 453

FIGURE 454

FIGURE 455

FIGURE 456

FIGURE 457

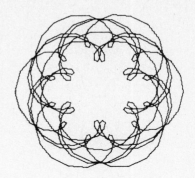

FIGURE 458

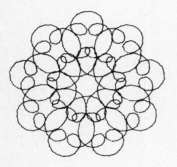

FIGURE 459

FIGURE 460

FIGURE 461

FIGURE 462

FIGURE 463

FIGURE 464

FIGURE 465

FIGURE 466

FIGURE 467

FIGURE 468

FIGURE 469

FIGURE 470

FIGURE 471

FIGURE 472

FIGURE 473

FIGURE 474

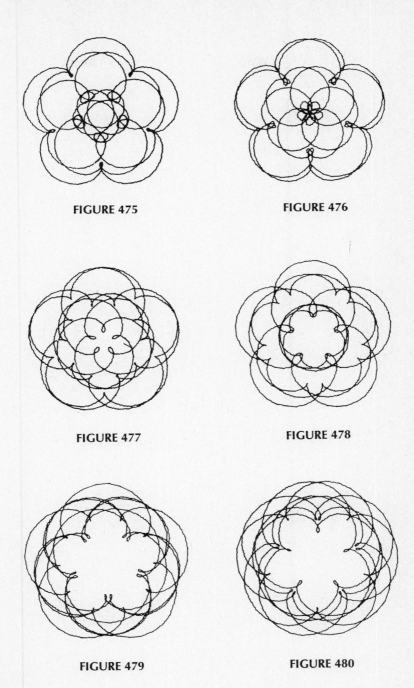

FIGURE 475

FIGURE 476

FIGURE 477

FIGURE 478

FIGURE 479

FIGURE 480

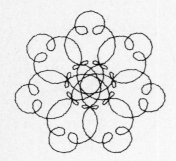

FIGURE 481

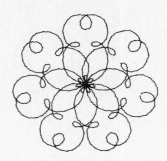

FIGURE 482

FIGURE 483

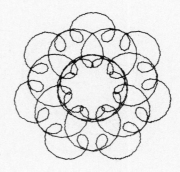

FIGURE 484

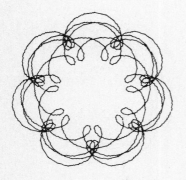

FIGURE 485

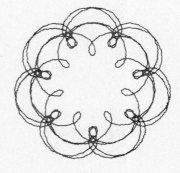

FIGURE 486

FIGURE 487

FIGURE 488

FIGURE 489

FIGURE 490

FIGURE 491

FIGURE 492

FIGURE 493

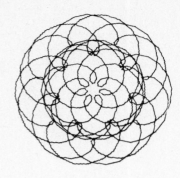

FIGURE 494

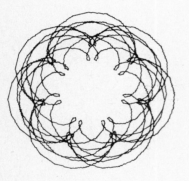

FIGURE 495

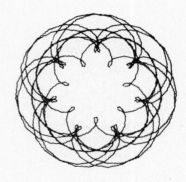

FIGURE 496

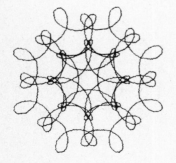

FIGURE 497

FIGURE 498

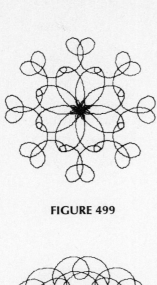
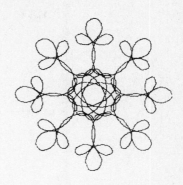

FIGURE 499

FIGURE 500

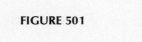

FIGURE 501

FIGURE 502

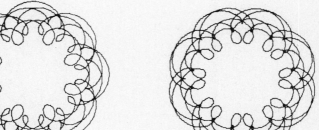

FIGURE 503

FIGURE 504

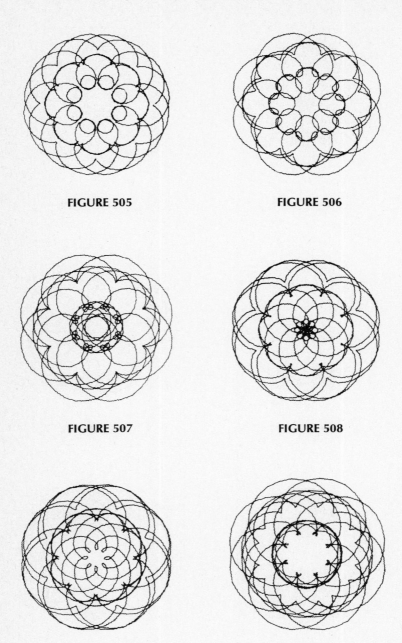

FIGURE 505

FIGURE 506

FIGURE 507

FIGURE 508

FIGURE 509

FIGURE 510

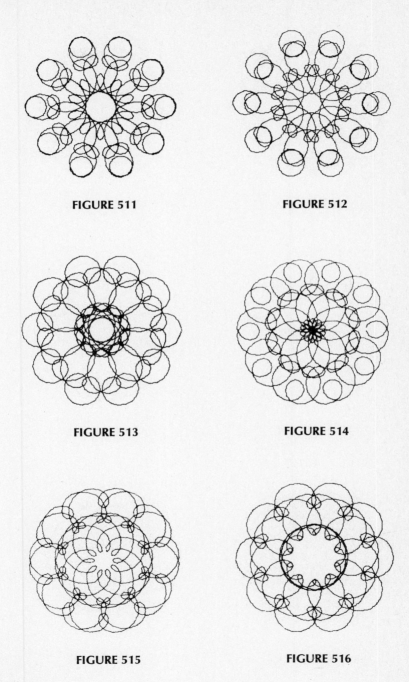

FIGURE 511

FIGURE 512

FIGURE 513

FIGURE 514

FIGURE 515

FIGURE 516

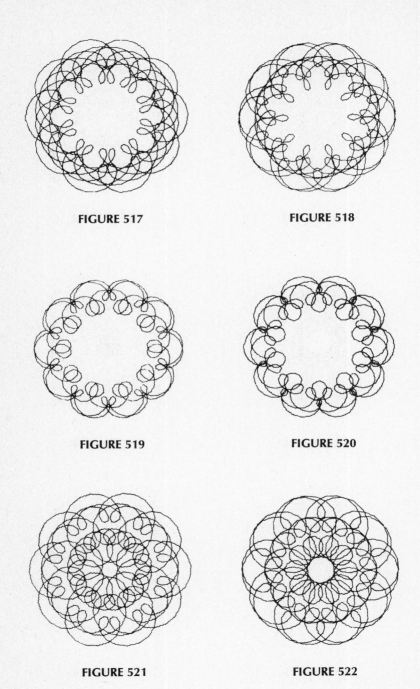

FIGURE 517   FIGURE 518

FIGURE 519   FIGURE 520

FIGURE 521   FIGURE 522

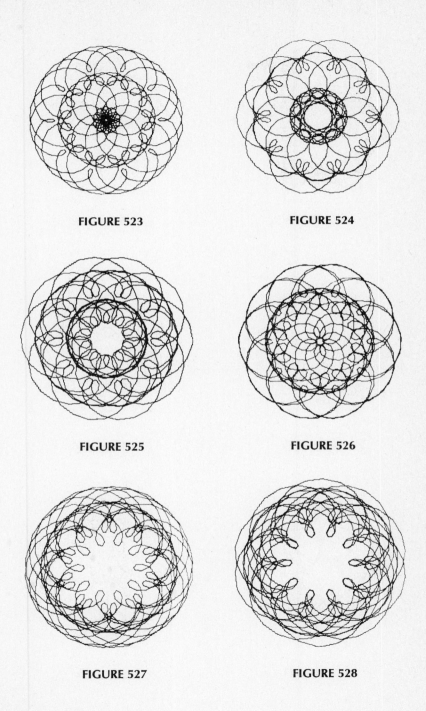

FIGURE 523

FIGURE 524

FIGURE 525

FIGURE 526

FIGURE 527

FIGURE 528

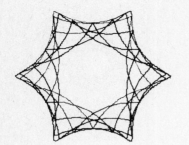

FIGURE 529

FIGURE 530

FIGURE 531

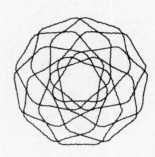

FIGURE 532

FIGURE 533

FIGURE 534

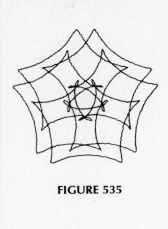

FIGURE 535

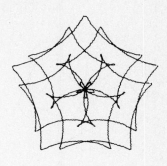

FIGURE 536

FIGURE 537

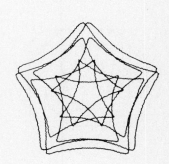

FIGURE 538

FIGURE 539

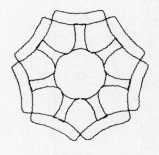

FIGURE 540

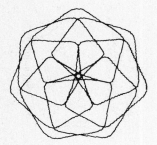

FIGURE 541

FIGURE 542

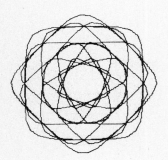

FIGURE 543

FIGURE 544

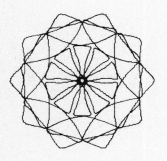

FIGURE 545

FIGURE 546

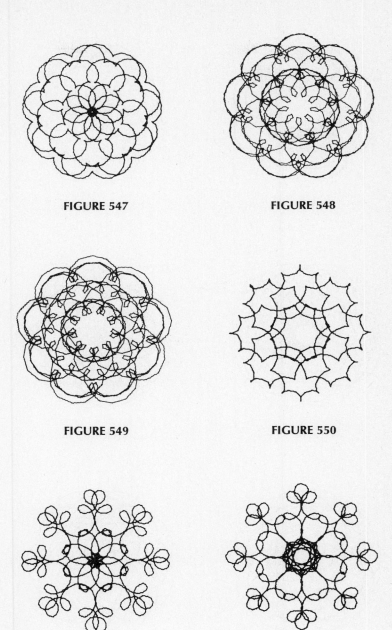

FIGURE 547

FIGURE 548

FIGURE 549

FIGURE 550

FIGURE 551

FIGURE 552

FIGURE 553

FIGURE 554

FIGURE 555

FIGURE 556

FIGURE 557

FIGURE 558

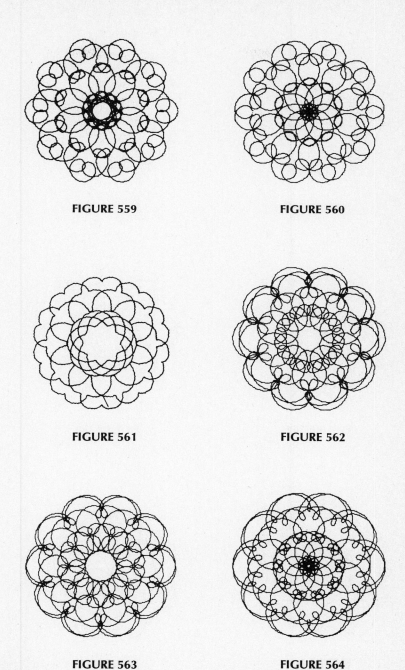

FIGURE 559

FIGURE 560

FIGURE 561

FIGURE 562

FIGURE 563

FIGURE 564

FIGURE 565

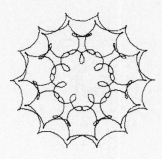

FIGURE 566

FIGURE 567

FIGURE 568

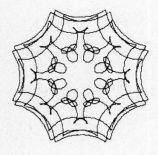

FIGURE 569

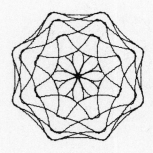

FIGURE 570

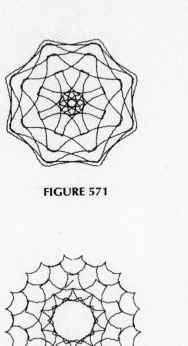

FIGURE 571

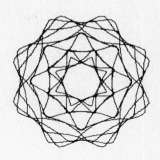

FIGURE 572

FIGURE 573

FIGURE 574

FIGURE 575

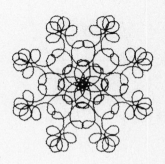

FIGURE 576

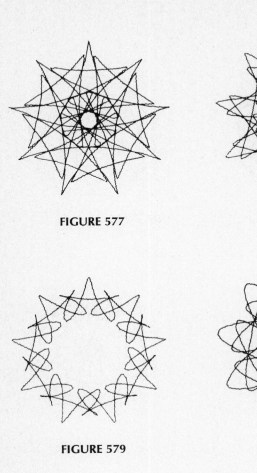

FIGURE 577

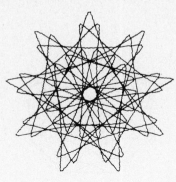

FIGURE 578

FIGURE 579

FIGURE 580

FIGURE 581

FIGURE 582

FIGURE 583

FIGURE 584

FIGURE 585

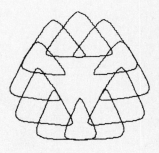

FIGURE 586

FIGURE 587

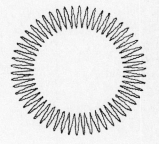

FIGURE 588

FIGURE 589

FIGURE 590

FIGURE 591

FIGURE 592

FIGURE 593

FIGURE 594

FIGURE 595

FIGURE 596

FIGURE 597

9 Speed Plotting

Reverend Savory states of the Geometric Lathe, "the general amount of time taken in cutting figures . . . [is] from ¼ of a minute to 5 minutes."

It is relatively easy to estimate the time it will take for the computer to generate any pattern. This will depend on two factors:

- Length of program loop
- Step size between dots.

For example, a pattern requiring a program length of $2*\pi$ with a step size of .05, will have $2*\pi/.05 = 125$ dots. The 8-bit personal computer we used plots at approximately four dots per second. Accordingly, it will take approximately $125/4 = 31$ seconds to plot this pattern.

Similarly a pattern such as Figure 594 will have $2*\pi/.001 = 6283$ dots. Accordingly, it will take the computer approximately 26 minutes to plot the pattern.

Let us now consider how it is possible to reduce plotting time by up to four times in a way that would have made Victorian Geometric Lathe operators extremely envious!

One of the interesting features of epicyclic patterns is that they are formed by one continuous line or a series of dots representing a continuous line (excluding, of course, the detailed patterns in Chapter 7). More important, however, is the fact that patterns formed (whether simple or compound) are symmetrical.

We can use these properties of continuity and symmetry to considerable advantage for it is possible to eliminate many of the calculations carried out by the computer. Consider the following Cartesian diagram:

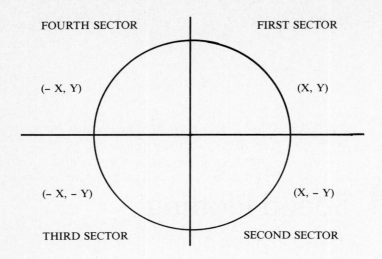

It can be seen here that the top half of the circle is the same as the bottom half and that the left half is the same as the right half. Accordingly, the x and y co-ordinates of a point on the circle in the first sector are exactly the same as those of a point on the circle in the second sector, with a change of sign (negative) of the y co-ordinate. The co-ordinates of points in the third and fourth sectors are similarly the same with only a change in sign (positive or negative).

We can now use symmetry to speed up the plotting process, by plotting four points from the one set of calculations carried out by the computer.

Consider Figure 143. In this case, our coefficients are:

R = 20 : S = 40 : T = 19
N = − 5 : M = 7

The program to generate the pattern is:

```
10   HCOLOR
14   R = 20 : S = 40 : T = 19
15   N = −5 : M = 7
20   FOR A = 0 TO 2*π STEP .01
30   X = R*COS(A) + S*COS(N*A) + T*COS(M*A) + 100
40   Y = R*SIN(A) + S*SIN(N*A) + T*SIN(M*A) + 100
50   PLOT X,Y
60   NEXT A
```

Let us now insert the following program lines:

```
51   PLOT 200 – X,Y
52   PLOT 200 – X, 200 – Y
53   PLOT X, 200 – Y
```

It will be seen that when the numeral 100 is used above, in calculating the values of x and y in lines 30 and 40, the computer has added 100 to each in order to center the pattern on the screen.

In order to plot symmetrical points above and below the horizontal (x) axis (which in itself is 100 units high), it is necessary to use the following instructions:

Plot x,y   (Point in first sector)
Plot x, 200 – y   (Point in second sector)

Similarly, to plot symmetrical points left and right of the vertical (y) axis (which in itself is 100 units to the right), it is necessary to use the following instructions:

Plot 200 – x, 200 – y   (Point in third sector)
Plot 200 – x, y   (Point in fourth sector)

Before running the program you should also amend line 20 to:

```
20   A = 0 TO 0.5*π STEP .01
```

Here it can be seen that if the computer is plotting four points simultaneously, it is only necessary for the program to be one-quarter as long as previously.

You may now run the program and see the speed at which the program is drawn (46 seconds on our computer compared to 165 seconds previously).

Unfortunately the foregoing principles apply only where patterns are symmetrical around both the horizontal and vertical axes. This applies to all patterns where the number of loops or cusps is even. However, where the number of loops or cusps is not even, the pattern will be symmetrical only around one axis.

Consider Figure 594. This pattern is symmetrical only around the x axis. Accordingly, we can plot only two symmetrical points simultaneously, being the points in the first and second sectors. The program necessary to generate the pattern is therefore:

```
10   HCOLOR
15   R = 48 : S = 32 : T = 12.8
16   N = –54 : M = 110
20   FOR A = 0 TO 1*π STEP .001
30   X = R*COS(A) + S*COS(N*A) + T*COS(M*A) + 100
49   Y = R*SIN(A) + S*SIN(N * A) + T*SIN(M*A) + 100
50   PLOT X,Y
60   PLOT X, 200 – Y
70   NEXT A
```

While this may not be as fast as plotting four points simultaneously, it is a vast improvement over plotting only one point at a time. (Plotting time on our computer was 14 minutes compared to 26 minutes previously.)

All epicyclic patterns are symmetrical about at least one axis, so that it is possible to apply the latter technique to all the patterns in this book.

It will be apparent that the principles involved in speeding up the plotting process require reducing the number of calculations to be completed by the computer. With some computers it is possible to save a high-resolution display on tape or disk. In reproducing the display, no computer time will be used in detailed calculations. Accordingly, the plotting time will be extremely fast. The saving of high-resolution displays is beyond the scope of this book and you should consult your own computer manual for more information.

10 Line Plotting

The method of drawing a pattern by plotting pixels along the length of the curve has several advantages:

- It is faster than plotting a continuous curve.
- It results in better (apparent) resolution in that the eye tends to fill in the curved path between pixels.

It is readily apparent that any pattern can be plotted as a continuous curve by merely decreasing the step size in the program loop to make pixels so close together that they appear to touch. However, the plotting would be rather time-consuming.

A faster method is to program the computer to draw successive lines between adjacent pixels. The procedure therefore involves drawing many small lines to appear as one continuous line. Here there is an obvious trade-off between drawing a line pattern quickly and drawing it with smooth, round curves. The larger the step size in the program loop, the shorter the time taken to plot the curve. But as each line segment will be longer, the result will be a less smooth curve.

With simple patterns you will have discovered that a step size of between .1 and .05 is generally satisfactory in plotting simple epicyclic curves using pixel points. The larger step size (.1) is satisfactory for more confined patterns; the smaller step size (.05) is necessary for patterns with large rounded loops.

Similarly with compound patterns, a step size of between .01 and .001 is generally satisfactory, depending on the nature of the pattern involved.

These guidelines are equally applicable to line plotting, so that the time taken to plot a pattern will be similar under either plotting method.

The program necessary to generate a line pattern depends on the type of computer used. Two types of instruction seem to be common.

1. Some computers plot lines by use of an instruction such as PLOT TO. In this case the relevant program will be of the following general form:

```
10   HCOLOR
15   R =  : S =  : T =
16   N =  : M =
20   FOR A = 0 TO 2*π STEP .01
30   X = R*COS(A) + S*COS(N*A) + T*COS(M*A) + 100
40   Y = R*SIN(A) + S*SIN(N*A) + T*SIN(M*A) + 100
50   IF Z = 1 THEN 80
60   PLOT X, Y
70   Z = 1
80   PLOT TO X,Y
90   NEXT A
```

It will be noted that before PLOT TO may be used to draw a line segment, it is necessary that PLOT or a previous PLOT TO provides a point for the beginning of the line segment. In the above program, you will see that the use of Z results in line 60 being used on the first execution of the program loop only. Having plotted the initial point, the computer will execute line 80 to draw successive lines.

2. Some computers plot lines by use of an instruction such as DRAW x_1, y_1, x_2, y_2. In this case x_1, y_1 are the co-ordinates of the start of a line and x_2, y_2 are the co-ordinates of the end of the line. The relevant program will be of the following general form:

```
10   H COLOR
15   R =  : S =  : T =
16   N = : M =
20   FOR A = 0 TO 2*π STEP .1
30   X₁ = R*COS(A) + S*COS(N*A) + T*COS(M*A) + 100
40   Y₁ = R*SIN(A) + S*SIN(N*A) + T*SIN(M*A) + 100
50   X₂ = R*COS(A+.1) + S*COS (N*(A+.1)) +
     T*COS(M*(A +.1)) + 100
60   Y₂ = R*SIN(A+.1) + S*SIN(N*(A+.1)) +
     T*SIN(M*(A+.1)) + 100
70   Draw X₁, Y₁, X₂, Y₂
80   NEXT A
```

This program can be improved upon, reducing the number of calculations done by the computer, as follows:

```
10   HCOLOR
15   R =  : S =  : T =
16   N =  : M =
20   FOR A = 0 TO 2*π STEP .1
25   IF Z = 1 THEN 50
30   X₂ = R*COS(A) + S*COS(N*A) + T*COS(M*A) + 100
40   Y₂ = R*SIN(A) + S*SIN (N*A) + T*SIN(M*A) + 100
45   Z = 1
50   X₁ = R*COS(A+.1) + S*COS(N*(A+.1)) +
     T*COS(M*(A+.1)) + 100
60   Y₁= R*SIN(A+.1) + S*SIN(N*(A+.1)) +
     T*SIN(M*(A+.1)) + 100
70   Draw X₁, Y₁, X₂, Y₂
75   X₁ = X₂ : Y₁ = Y₂
80   NEXT A
```

By way of interest, our computer completed the line drawing of Figure 292 in 30 seconds. Using the improved program above, the computer completed the pattern in 17 seconds.

Needless to say, the above programs are fairly slow, but they can be speeded up using the principles of symmetry explained in the previous chapter, drawing two or four lines simultaneously between points with co-ordinates of the same absolute numerical value but of different sign (positive or negative).

11 Plotting Advanced Compound Epicyclic Patterns

In changing from simple to compound patterns, you will note that the addition of a small epicyclic wheel to the Geometric Lathe results in generating the same simple pattern in an embellished form. For example, Figure 598 is generated from the simple program outlined in Chapter 5, as follows:

```
10   HCOLOR
15   R = 38.4 : S = 21.6
16   N = -4/3
20   FOR A = 0 TO 6*π STEP .1
30   X = R*COS(A) + S*COS(N*A) + 100
40   Y = R*SIN(A) + S*SIN(N*A) + 100
50   PLOT X,Y
60   NEXT A
```

The same embellished pattern is generated from the compound program outlined in Chapter 8, as follows for Figure 599:

```
10   HCOLOR
15   R = 38.4 : S = 21.6 : T = 6
16   N = -4/3 : M = 31
20   FOR A = 0 TO 6*π STEP .01
30   X = R*COS(A) + S*COS(N*A) + T*COS(M*A) + 100
40   Y = R*SIN(A) + S*SIN(N*A) + T*SIN(M*A) + 100
50   PLOT X,Y
60   NEXT A
```

You will recall that the sum of the coefficients R, S, and T equals the radius of the pattern. To increase or decrease the size of a pattern, R, S, and T must be increased or decreased in the same proportion.

The same principle can now be adopted in changing from compound to advanced compound epicyclic patterns. The latter are generated by adding a further small epicyclic wheel to the Geometric Lathe. For example, Figure 600 is generated from the general compound program outlined in Chapter 8:

```
10   HCOLOR
15   R = 40 : S = 20 : T = 15
16   N = -3 : M = 5
20   FOR A = 0 TO 2*π STEP .01
30   X = R*COS(A) + S*COS(N*A) + T*COS(M*A) + 100
40   Y = R*SIN(A) + S*SIN(N*A) + T*SIN(M*A) + 100
50   PLOT X,Y
60   NEXT A
```

The same embellished pattern is generated from the advanced compound program as follows for Figure 601:

```
10   HCOLOR
15   R = 40 : S = 20 : T = 15 : U = 20
16   N = -3 : M = 5 : L = 100
20   FOR A = 0 TO 2*π STEP .001
30   X = R*COS(A) + S*COS(N*A) + T*COS(M*A) +
     U*COS(L*A) + 100
40   Y = R*SIN(A) + S*SIN(N*A) + T*SIN(M*A) +
     U*SIN(L*A) + 100
50   PLOT X,Y
60   NEXT A
```

In generating this pattern, apply the principles of symmetry outlined in Chapter 9 in order to speed up the plotting process.

Similarly, it will be noted that Figure 602 is generated from the following coefficients:

```
15   R = 63 : S = 14 : T = 17.5
16   N = -17 : M = 19
20   FOR A = 0 TO 2*π STEP .01
```

And Figure 603:

```
15   R = 63 : S = 14 : T = 17.5 : U =10.5
16   N = -17 : M = 19 : L = 1000
20   FOR A = 0 TO 2*π STEP .0005
```

The pattern in Figure 603 is too detailed for the limited resolution of the screen of a small personal computer. However, it can be plotted satisfactorily on a plotter printer. (You should increase the values of R, S, T, and U to enlarge the pattern to the maximum size acceptable on the printer.)

In printing this pattern you will have to be patient. Unfortunately, the printer is unable to plot more than one point at a time and, therefore, the principles of symmetry cannot be applied. The pattern will take more than two hours to print. You may also like to compare Figures 604 and 605. Figure 604 is generated from the following coefficients:

```
15   R = 54 : S = 12 : T = 18
16   N = 16 : M = -14
20   FOR A = 0 TO 2*π STEP .01
```

And Figure 605:

```
15   R = 54 : S = 12 : T = 18 : U = 12
16   N = 16 : M = -14 : L = 600
20   FOR A = 0 TO 2*π STEP .0005
```

As with the proceeding patterns, you will note that the difference between the foundation pattern (Figure 604) and the embellished pattern (Figure 605) is the addition of a further epicyclic wheel represented by the coefficients U and L. Note also with Figures 603 and 605 that the larger the value of L, the more rotations of the last epicyclic wheel and hence more detail in the pattern.

Other examples of overlaying circles on a compound pattern are as follows:

Figure 606:

```
15   R = 40 : S = 20 : T = 12
16   N= -5 : M = 19
```

Figure 607:

15 R = 51 : S = 24 : T = 15 : U 3.6
16 N = -5 : M = 19 : L = 1000

Figure 608:

15 R = 40 : S = 20 : T = -7
16 N = 10 : M = 17

Figure 609:

15 R = 50 : S = 25 : T = -9.5 : U = -3.5
16 N = 10 : M = -17 : L = 1000

Figures 610 to 632 demonstrate the effect of overlaying loops rather than circles on a compound pattern. It would appear that Victorian Geometric Lathe engravers developed such advanced compound patterns by first selecting a suitable foundation curve and then embellishing it.

Bazley states:

> It is needless to multiply examples of four-part turning: the few now given are sufficent to prove that the course of any two-part curve can be clothed with a repetition in distinct groups of any simple figure which the [lathe] can produce.

You will be able to develop advanced compound patterns in the same way. For example, Figures 615 and 617 appear to be part of a family of patterns each having a different number of major compartments, determined by their foundation curves, which are Figures 614 and 616. The latter are simple rectilinear curves developed in accordance with the rules outlined in Chapters 5 and 6.

You will see that the coefficients used here are larger than those used in the tables. This is merely because, in order to best highlight the intricate detail of these patterns, we have chosen the maximum coefficients acceptable on a 320 x 200 high-resolution computer screen. If your screen is smaller, you can scale down proportionately as previously described.

You will note that with some patterns, because of their elliptical shape, it is possible to use coefficients R, S, T, and U, whose sum exceeds the height radius of the computer screen. For example, with Figure 612, the sum of the coefficients R, S, T, and U, is 186 and with Figure 613, the sum is 142.6. The more circular the general shape of a pattern, the less scope exists to capitalize on this.

If you are using a plotter printer, you may choose to rotate patterns such as Figures 612 and 613 so that they are plotted vertically. By doing this it is possible to enlarge the patterns considerably more than by plotting them horizontally. The principle involved in doing this is as for compound patterns. As discussed in Chapter 8 it is necessary to transpose lines 30 and 40 of the general program, as follows:

30   X = R*SIN(A) + S*SIN(N*A) + T*SIN(M*A) + U*SIN(L*A) + 100
40   Y = R*COS(A) + S*COS(N*A) + T*COS(M*A) + U*COS(L*A) + 100

For screen patterns, you may use a step size of .0005 to obtain good resolution. However, you would best use the principles of symmetry to speed up the plotting process, as described in Chapter 9. For example, plotting these patterns with the step size of .0005, will involve the computer plotting $2* \pi/.005 = 12,566$ dots on your screen to complete the pattern.

Using a personal computer which plots around four dots per second will take 52 minutes to complete each pattern. Using symmetry it will be possible to reduce this time to 26 or even 13 minutes.

The following table gives coefficients to plot the patterns shown at the end of this chapter.

Fig.	R	S	T	U	N	M	L
610	38	22			-5/2		
611	45	27	6	-13.8	-5/2	-415/2	405/2
612	105	30	18	-33	-1	159	-161
613	80.5	23	13.8	25.3	-1	159	-161
614	48	12			-2		
615	60	15	12	-18	-2	-189	185
616	54	6			-3		
617	72	8	9.6	-16	-3	-189	183
618	48.75	26	7.8	11.7	-3	-253	247
619	70	8.4	8.4	7.7	9	375	-357
620	75	6.75	9	7.7	-7	313	-327
621	67.5	10.5	11.25	-10.5	-7	249	-263
622	70	7	8.4	-8.4	9	375	-357
623	60	24	14.4	13.6	-5	379	-365
624	60	24	14.25	-13.5	9	-375	369

Fig.	R	S	T	U	N	M	L
625	56	14.7	13.3	−12.6	−6	330	−321
626	56	10.4	16	18.4	−4	236	−229
627	56	14	12.6	11.9	−7	249	−247
628	56	21	7	−7.7	−7	249	−247
629	49	24.5	6.3	12.6	−5	251	−245
630	56	22.4	5.6	−9.8	6	−314	306
631	56	24.5	7.7	−7	7	331	−299
632	56	28	7	6.3	7	331	−299

Figures 633, 634, and 635, referred to in Elphinstone's book as a "true lovers' knot," illustrate the effect of overlaying circles and loops on the same foundation curve. Figure 633 is a compound pattern (generated with the use of two epicyclic wheels), Figure 634 is an advanced compound pattern (generated with three epicyclic wheels). Figure 635 is a further advanced compound pattern (generated with four epicyclic wheels).

You may ask how the Victorians were able to generate patterns such as the latter. In fact they were produced with the aid of *two* Geometric Lathes! One lathe held the engraving tool, the other held the object being engraved. Both the tool and the object rotated epicyclically to produce the advanced compound pattern.

Figure 633 is produced as follows:

```
15  R = 20.4 : S = 40.8 : T = 40.8
16  N = 3 : M = −1
```

Figure 634 is produced as follows:

```
15  R = 20.4 : S = 40.8 : T = 40.8 : U = 10.8
16  N = 3 : M = −1 : L = 192
```

Figure 635 is produced from a new mathematical formula, which reflects the use of a fourth epicyclic wheel, as follows:

```
30  X = R*COS(A) + S*COS(N*A) + T*COS(M*A) +
    U*COS(L*A) + V*COS(K*A) + 100
40  Y = R*SIN(A) + S*SIN(N*A) + T*SIN(M*A) +
    U*SIN(L*A) + V*SIN(K*A) + 100
```

The coefficients necessary for generating Figure 635 are as follows:

15   R = 20.4 : S = 40.8 : T = 40.8 : U = 14.4 : V = 14.4
16   N = 3 : M = –1 : L = 189 : K = –191

Coefficients for generating the remaining patterns are as follows:

Figure 636 (companion curve to Figure 635, the sign of V being the only difference in the coefficients):

15   R = 20.4 : S = 40.8 : T = 40.8 : U = 14.4 : V = – 14.4
16   N = 3 : M = –1 : L = 189 : K = –191

Figure 637 (foundation curve to Figure 638, the coefficients R, S, N, and M being the same):

15   R = 88 : S = 17.6 : T = –17.6
16   N = –1 : M = 11

Figure 638:

15   R = 88 : S = 17.6 : T = 11 : U = 9.9 : V = 7.7
16   N = –1 : M = 11 : L = 469 : K = –447

Figures 639 and 640 reflect the best or the worst of Victorian engraving (depending on your taste!). In discussing these patterns, being numbers 3499 and 3500 in his work, Bazley stated:

> The actual process of engraving these rather intricate fractional figures is a singular one. The curve, it will be remembered is single and continuous, and, for a considerable part of its course, the several portions of which it is (so far) composed appear discordant, and to have no prospect of forming a harmonious whole. But as the delineation proceeds, the irregular convolutions of the curve recur at such intervals as to overlap symmetrically, or to adopt such positions with reference to one another as to render the effect both complete and ornamental.

The coefficients necessary to generate these patterns are as follows:

Figure 639:

15   R = 60 : S = 22.5 : T = 18.75 : U = 5.625 : V = –5
16   N = –7 : M = 11 : L = 662 : K: = –592

Figure 640:

15   R = 47.5 : S = 15 : T = 15 : U = 4 : V = 3.5
16   N = –7 : M = 13 : L = 662 : K = –588

DETAILED COMPOUND PATTERNS

At this stage, you will have realised that there has been little discussion of detailed compound patterns, along the lines of detailed simple patterns as in Chapter 7. In most cases, little embellishment of compound patterns is necessary, but Figures 641 to 643 are a few examples. These are generated by the following coefficients:

Figure 641:

Inside pattern:
15   R = 32 : S = 11.2 : T = 11.2
16   N = 101/2 : M = –115/2

Outside pattern:
15   R = 72 : S = 12 : T = 10.4
16   N = 100 : M = –188

Figure 642:

Inside pattern:
15   R = 28 : S = 10.5 : T = 7.7
16   N = 163/3 : M = –145/3

Outside pattern:
15   R = 70 : S = 10.5 : T = 10.5
16   N = 179/3 : M = –239/3

Figure 643:

Inside pattern:
15   R = 32 : S = 14.4 : T = 14.4
16   N = 143/3 : M = –51

Outside pattern:

15   $R = 72 : S = 10.4 : T = 10.4$
16   $N = 223/3 : M = -67$

In these cases you will be able to plot inside and outside patterns in different colors if you wish.

Title page illustration:

15   $R = 60 : S = 22 : T = 20$
16   $N = 79/2 : M = -211/6$

In conclusion, we feel compelled to include an extract of a letter reported in *English Mechanic*, 27 April 1883, being eight years after the publication of Bazley's two books (which include a total of 3615 patterns). Bazley wrote, "I have not perpetrated a pattern since my books were finished." We feel a similar reluctance!

The enthusiastic reader, however, may well ask: "Where to now?" No doubt the reader of a book on the Geometric Lathe would have asked the same question more than one hundred years ago. Perhaps he would have been enlightened by the following dialog, from *Alice's Adventures in Wonderland and Through the Looking-Glass* (first published in 1865) by Lewis Carroll:

> The Cat grinned when it saw Alice. It looked good-natured, she thought: still it had *VERY* long claws and a great many teeth, so she felt that it ought to be treated with respect.
>
> 'Cheshire Puss,' she began, rather timidly, as she did not at all know whether it would like the name: however, it only grinned a little wider.
>
> 'Come, it's pleased so far,' thought Alice, and she went on. 'Would you tell me, please, which way I ought to go from here?'
>
> 'That depends a good deal on where you want to get to,' said the Cat.
>
> 'I don't much care where —' said Alice.
>
> 'Then it doesn't matter which way you go,' said the Cat.
>
> '— so long as I get SOMEWHERE,' Alice added as an explanation.
>
> 'Oh, you're sure to do that,' said the Cat, 'if you only walk long enough.'

FIGURE 598

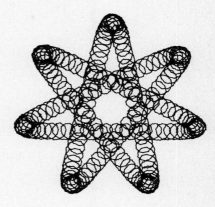

FIGURE 599

FIGURE 600

FIGURE 601

FIGURE 602

FIGURE 603

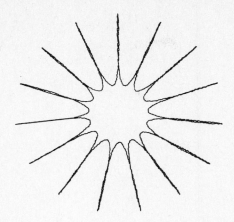

FIGURE 604

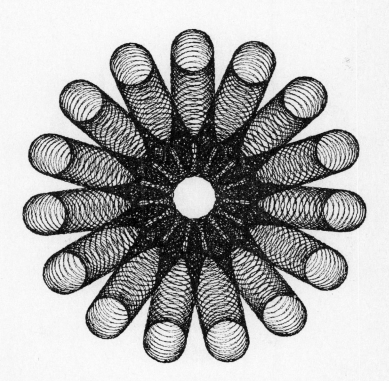

FIGURE 605

FIGURE 606

FIGURE 607

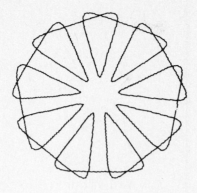

FIGURE 608

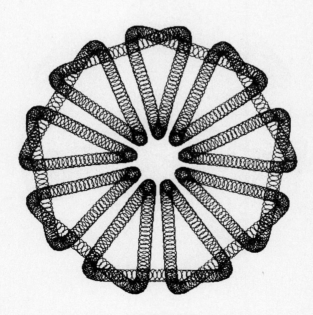

FIGURE 609

FIGURE 610

FIGURE 611

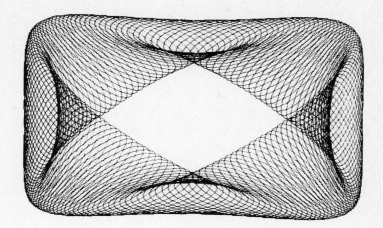

FIGURE 612

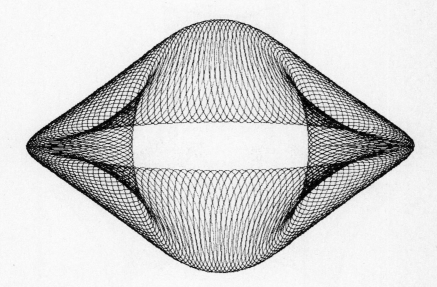

FIGURE 613

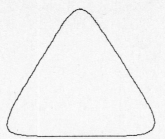

FIGURE 614

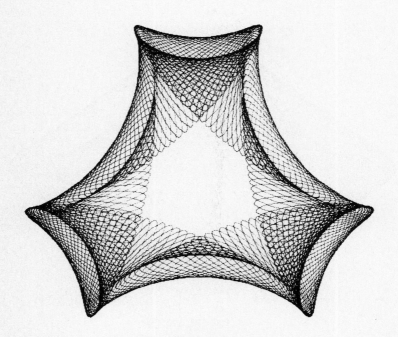

FIGURE 615

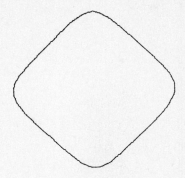

FIGURE 616

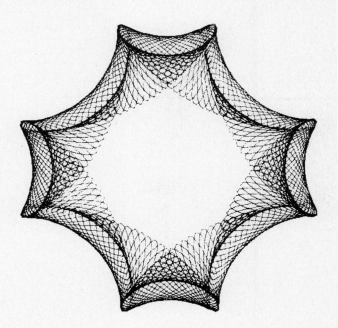

FIGURE 617

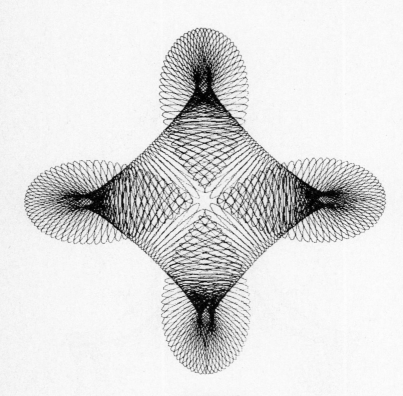

FIGURE 618

FIGURE 619

FIGURE 620

FIGURE 621

FIGURE 622

FIGURE 623

FIGURE 624

FIGURE 625

FIGURE 626

FIGURE 627

FIGURE 628

FIGURE 629

FIGURE 630

FIGURE 631

FIGURE 632

FIGURE 633

FIGURE 634

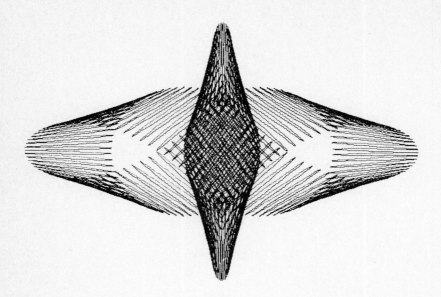

FIGURE 635

FIGURE 636

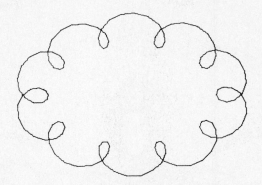

FIGURE 637

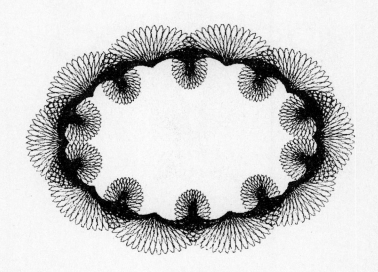

FIGURE 638

FIGURE 639

FIGURE 640

FIGURE 641

FIGURE 642

FIGURE 643

BIBLIOGRAPHY

G.B. Suardi, *Nuovi Instrumento per la Descrizione di diverse Curve Antichi e Moderne* (1752).

G. Adams, *Geometrical and Graphical Essays* (London, 1791).

L. Bergeron, *Manuel du Tourneur* (Paris, 1816)

J.H. Ibbetson, *A Brief Account of Ibbetson's Geometric Chuck* (London, 1833).

A. de Morgan, *Penny Cyclopaedia* (London, 1843)

J.H. Ibbetson, *Specimens in Eccentric Turning* (London, 1851).

W.F. Stanley, *A Treatise on Mathematical Drawing Instruments* (London, 1866).

H. Perigal, Numerous pamphlets on geometric patterns (London, c.1870).

T.S. Bazley, *Notes on the Epicycloidal Cutting Frame* (London, 1872).

H.W. Elphinstone, *Patterns for Turning* (London, 1872).

H.S. Savory, *Geometric Turning* (London, 1873).

T.S. Bazley, *Index to the Geometric Chuck* (London, 1875).

W.H. Northcott, *A Treatise on Lathes and Turning* (London, 1875).

R.A. Proctor, *A Treatise on the Cycloid* (London 1878).

J.J. Holtzapffel, *Principles and Practice of Ornamental or Complex Turning* (London, 1884).

APPENDIX

Table for Plotting Illustrated Compound Epicyclic Patterns

To plot illustrated patterns, insert numerical values of coefficients R, S, T, N, and M in lines 15 and 16 of general program set out in Chapter 8.

Fig.	R	S	T	N	M	Suggested Step Size
85	20	40	18	4	7	.025
86	30	30	16	−3	−7	.025
87	20	40	13	−3	−7	.025
88	30	30	19	5	9	.025
89	20	40	13	5	9	.025
90	30	30	14	−5	11	.025
91	50	10	10	7	13	.025
92	40	20	−13	7	13	.015
93	30	30	15	7	13	.015
94	40	20	10	−8	−17	.015
95	40	20	−10	−8	−17	.015
96	30	30	15	−8	−17	.015
97	50	10	−10	10	19	.01
98	40	20	14	10	19	.01
99	30	30	20	10	19	.01
100	40	20	−9	−3/2	−4	.05
101	30	30	15	−3/2	−4	.05
102	20	40	15	−3/2	−4	.05
103	40	20	13	7/2	6	.025
104	30	30	22	7/2	6	.025
105	40	20	13	−5/2	−6	.035
106	30	30	4	−5/2	−6	.035
107	40	20	−16	9/2	8	.025
108	30	30	20	9/2	8	.025
109	50	10	−8	−3/5	−11/5	.05
110	50	10	10	−3/5	−11/5	.05
111	50	10	20	−3/5	−11/5	.05
112	50	10	−22	−3/5	−11/5	.05
113	40	20	10	−3/5	−11/5	.05
114	40	20	−10	−3/5	−11/5	.05
115	40	20	23	−3/5	−11/5	.05
116	30	30	−10	−3/5	−11/5	.05
117	30	30	18	−3/5	−11/5	.05
118	20	40	10	−3/5	−11/5	.05
119	10	50	−15	−3/5	−11/5	.05

Fig.	R	S	T	N	M	Suggested Step Size
120	50	10	−17	13/5	21/5	.05
121	40	20	8	13/5	21/5	.05
122	30	30	15	13/5	21/5	.05
123	50	10	−5	−7/3	−17/3	.025
124	40	20	3	−7/3	−17/3	.025
125	40	20	−3	−7/3	−17/3	.025
126	40	20	15	−7/3	−17/3	.025
127	30	30	13	−7/3	−17/3	.025
128	20	40	6	−7/3	−17/3	.025
129	10	50	−20	−7/3	−17/3	.025
130	50	10	6	13/3	23/3	.025
131	50	10	−6	13/3	23/3	.025
132	50	10	−13	13/3	23/3	.025
133	40	20	15	13/3	23/3	.025
134	30	30	20	13/3	23/3	.025
135	40	20	15	−3	5	.035
136	30	30	11	−3	5	.035
137	20	40	−15	−3	5	.035
138	20	40	15	−3	5	.035
139	10	50	15	5	−3	.025
140	40	20	15	−5	7	.025
141	30	30	15	−5	7	.025
142	30	30	25	−5	7	.025
143	20	40	19	−5	7	.025
144	50	10	20	7	−5	.025
145	40	20	15	7	−5	.025
146	30	30	20	7	−5	.025
147	50	10	12	−8	10	.015
148	40	20	5	−8	10	.015
149	40	20	−5	−8	10	.015
150	40	20	17	−8	10	.015
151	30	30	−11	−8	10	.015
152	30	30	18	−8	10	.015
153	20	40	15	−8	10	.015
154	20	40	15	−8	10	.015

Fig.	R	S	T	N	M	Suggested Step Size
155	50	10	6	10	−8	.01
156	50	10	15	10	−8	.01
157	40	20	7	10	−8	.01
158	30	30	20	10	−8	.01
159	20	40	20	10	−8	.01
160	20	40	−20	10	−8	.01
161	30	30	−10	−3/2	7/2	.01
162	40	20	15	−3/2	7/2	.01
163	20	40	−10	−3/2	7/2	.01
164	20	40	10	−3/2	7/2	.01
165	25	40	9	−3/2	7/2	.01
166	40	20	10	7/2	−3/2	.01
167	40	20	−10	7/2	−3/2	.025
168	30	30	20	7/2	−3/2	.025
169	30	30	−20	7/2	−3/2	.025
170	50	10	10	−5/2	9/2	.025
171	50	10	−20	−5/2	9/2	.025
172	40	20	5	−5/2	9/2	.025
173	40	20	10	−5/2	9/2	.025
174	30	30	−6	−5/2	9/2	.025
175	30	30	6	−5/2	9/2	.025
176	20	40	−10	−5/2	9/2	.025
177	20	40	10	−5/2	9/2	.025
178	10	50	12	−5/2	9/2	.025
179	50	10	20	9/2	−5/2	.025
180	50	10	−35	9/2	−5/2	.025
181	40	20	15	9/2	−5/2	.025
182	30	30	25	9/2	−5/2	.025
183	20	40	−20	9/2	−5/2	.025
184	20	40	38	9/2	−5/2	.025
185	30	30	20	−3/5	13/5	.075
186	20	40	1	−3/5	13/5	.075
187	20	40	−6	−3/5	13/5	.075
188	20	40	19	−3/5	13/5	.075
189	20	40	−19	−3/5	13/5	.075

Fig.	R	S	T	N	M	Suggested Step Size
190	10	50	−5	−3/5	13/5	.075
191	10	50	5	−3/5	13/5	.075
192	20	40	22	13/5	−3/5	.025
193	20	40	−22	13/5	−3/5	.025
194	50	10	−20	−7/3	13/3	.025
195	40	20	5	−7/3	13/3	.025
196	40	20	10	−7/3	13/3	.025
197	30	30	9	−7/3	13/3	.025
198	30	30	−9	−7/3	13/3	.025
199	30	30	21	−7/3	13/3	.025
200	20	40	10	−7/3	13/3	.025
201	20	40	−10	−7/3	13/3	.025
202	20	40	25	−7/3	13/3	.025
203	20	40	−22	−7/3	13/3	.025
204	10	50	−22	−7/3	13/3	.025
205	50	10	25	13/3	−7/3	.025
206	50	10	−25	13/3	−7/3	.025
207	50	10	−35	13/3	−7/3	.025
208	40	20	−10	13/3	−7/3	.025
209	30	30	25	13/3	−7/3	.025
210	20	40	20	13/3	−7/3	.025
211	20	40	−20	13/3	−7/3	.025
212	40	20	15	7	19	.01
213	20	40	10	7	19	.01
214	40	20	15	−8	−26	.01
215	30	30	−11	−8	−26	.01
216	30	30	11	−8	−26	.01
217	40	20	12	10	28	.01
218	40	20	−12	10	28	.01
219	40	20	17	17/2	17/2	.025
220	30	30	−15	7/2	17/2	.025
221	40	20	8	−5/2	−19/2	.025
222	30	30	10	−5/2	−19/2	.025
223	20	40	10	−5/2	−19/2	.025
224	20	40	−10	−5/2	−19/2	.025

Fig.	R	S	T	N	M	Suggested Step Size
225	10	50	−18	−5/2	−19/2	.025
226	10	50	18	−5/2	−19/2	.025
227	40	20	12	9/2	23/2	.025
228	20	40	17	9/2	23/2	.025
229	50	10	4	−3/5	−19/5	.05
230	50	10	−4	−3/5	−19/5	.05
231	50	10	9	−3/5	−19/5	.05
232	50	10	−9	−3/5	−19/5	.05
233	40	20	3	−3/5	−19/5	.075
234	40	20	−3	−3/5	−19/5	.075
235	30	30	−4	−3/5	−19/5	.075
236	30	30	4	−3/5	−19/5	.075
237	20	40	15	−3/5	−19/5	.075
238	10	50	−10	−3/5	−19/5	.075
239	10	50	10	−3/5	−19/5	.075
240	50	10	−10	13/5	29/5	.025
241	40	20	−15	13/5	29/5	.025
242	40	20	15	13/5	29/5	.025
243	20	40	18	13/5	29/5	.025
244	40	20	11	−7/3	−9	.025
245	30	30	7	−7/3	−9	.025
246	20	40	10	−7/3	−9	.025
247	50	10	8	13/3	11	.015
248	40	20	−13	13/3	11	.015
249	40	20	13	13/3	11	.015
250	30	30	13	13/3	11	.015
251	20	40	13	13/3	11	.015
252	30	30	−8	−3	9	.015
253	30	30	8	5	−7	.015
254	30	30	−8	5	−7	.015
255	30	30	−15	5	−7	.015
256	20	40	−23	5	−7	.015
257	30	30	−9	−5	13	.015
258	30	30	9	−5	13	.015
259	20	40	−5	−5	13	.015

Fig.	R	S	T	N	M	Suggested Step Size
260	20	40	5	−5	13	.015
261	20	40	13	−5	13	.015
262	20	40	−13	−5	13	.015
263	40	20	−8	7	−11	.015
264	40	20	8	7	−11	.015
265	40	20	−14	7	−11	.015
266	40	20	14	7	−11	.015
267	30	30	−14	7	−11	.015
268	20	40	17	7	−11	.015
269	40	20	−5	−8	19	.01
270	40	20	5	−8	19	.01
271	30	30	6	−8	19	.01
272	30	30	−6	−8	19	.01
273	30	30	−12	−8	19	.01
274	30	30	12	−8	19	.01
275	30	30	−18	−8	19	.01
276	30	30	18	−8	19	.01
277	20	40	−10	−8	19	.01
278	20	40	10	−8	19	.01
279	40	20	−7	10	−17	.01
280	40	20	7	10	−17	.01
281	40	20	−12	10	−17	.01
282	40	20	20	10	−17	.01
283	30	30	10	10	−17	.01
284	30	30	−10	10	−17	.01
285	30	30	19	10	−17	.01
286	30	30	−19	10	−17	.01
287	20	40	19	10	−17	.01
288	40	20	20	7/2	−4	.025
289	30	30	7	−5/2	8	.025
290	30	30	−7	−5/2	8	.025
291	20	40	7	−5/2	8	.025
292	20	40	−7	−5/2	8	.025
293	20	40	15	−5/2	8	.025
294	40	20	−15	9/2	−6	.025

Fig.	R	S	T	N	M	Suggested Step Size
295	40	20	20	9/2	−6	.025
296	30	30	−16	9/2	−6	.025
297	20	40	19	9/2	−6	.025
298	20	40	−19	9/2	−6	.025
299	10	50	19	9/2	−6	.025
300	30	30	−15	−3/5	21/5	.05
301	30	30	15	−3/5	21/5	.05
302	20	40	9	−3/5	21/5	.05
303	50	10	−15	13/5	−11/5	.05
304	50	10	20	13/5	−11/5	.05
305	50	10	−25	13/5	−11/5	.05
306	40	20	20	13/5	−11/5	.05
307	30	30	21	13/5	−11/5	.05
308	30	30	−21	13/5	−11/5	.05
309	20	40	21	13/5	−11/5	.05
310	50	10	16	−7/3	23/3	.025
311	50	10	−16	−7/3	23/3	.025
312	40	20	16	−7/3	23/3	.025
313	30	30	14	−7/3	23/3	.025
314	30	30	−14	−7/3	23/3	.025
315	20	40	−17	−7/3	23/3	.025
316	20	40	17	−7/3	23/3	.025
317	10	50	20	−7/3	23/3	.025
318	50	10	13	13/3	−17/3	.015
319	50	10	−13	13/3	−17/3	.015
320	40	20	−10	13/3	−17/3	.015
321	40	20	9	13/3	−17/3	.015
322	30	30	16	13/3	−17/3	.015
323	30	30	−16	13/3	−17/3	.015
324	20	40	−22	13/3	−17/3	.015
325	20	40	22	13/3	−17/3	.015
326	10	50	20	5	17	.01
327	10	50	−20	5	17	.01
328	30	30	15	−5	−23	.01
329	30	30	−15	−5	−23	.01

Fig.	R	S	T	N	M	Suggested Step Size
330	20	40	−15	−5	−23	.01
331	20	40	15	−5	−23	.01
332	10	50	15	−5	−23	.01
333	10	50	−15	−5	−23	.01
334	10	50	−15	7	25	.01
335	10	50	15	7	25	.005
336	40	20	−12	−8	−35	.005
337	40	20	12	−8	−35	.005
338	30	30	12	−8	−35	.005
339	30	30	−12	−8	−35	.005
340	20	40	−14	−8	−35	.005
341	20	40	14	−8	−35	.005
342	10	50	−16	−8	−35	.005
343	10	50	16	−8	−35	.005
344	40	20	10	10	37	.005
345	40	20	−10	10	37	.005
346	30	30	12	−5/2	−13	.015
347	30	30	−12	−5/2	−13	.015
348	20	40	−12	−5/2	−13	.015
349	20	40	12	−5/2	−13	.015
350	10	50	15	−5/2	−13	.015
351	10	50	−15	−5/2	−13	.015
352	40	20	14	9/2	15	.01
353	40	20	−14	9/2	15	.01
354	20	40	15	9/2	15	.01
355	20	40	−15	37/5	9/2	.01
356	40	20	15	37/5	13/5	.025
357	40	20	−15	37/5	13/5	.025
358	30	30	−15	37/5	13/5	.025
359	30	30	15	37/5	13/5	.025
360	30	30	15	−7/3	−37/3	.015
361	30	30	−15	−7/3	−37/3	.015
362	20	40	−15	−7/3	−37/3	.015
363	20	40	15	−7/3	−37/3	.015
364	10	50	15	−7/3	−37/3	.015

Fig.	R	S	T	N	M	Suggested Step Size
365	50	10	12	13/3	43/3	.015
366	40	20	12	13/3	43/3	.015
367	40	20	−12	13/3	43/3	.015
368	30	30	16	13/3	43/3	.015
369	20	40	15	13/3	43/3	.015
370	50	10	10	5	−11	.015
371	50	10	−10	5	−11	.015
372	40	20	5	5	−11	.015
373	40	20	−5	5	−11	.015
374	30	30	−11	5	−11	.015
375	30	30	11	5	−11	.015
376	20	40	17	5	−11	.015
377	20	40	−17	5	−11	.015
378	10	50	−20	5	−11	.015
379	10	50	20	5	−11	.015
380	40	20	−12	−5	19	.01
381	40	20	12	−5	19	.01
382	30	30	12	−5	19	.01
383	30	30	−12	−5	19	.01
384	20	40	10	−5	19	.01
385	20	40	−10	−5	19	.01
386	40	20	−15	7	−17	.01
387	40	20	15	7	−17	.01
388	30	30	15	7	−17	.01
389	30	30	−15	7	−17	.01
390	20	40	−15	7	−17	.01
391	20	40	15	7	−17	.01
392	40	20	−11	−8	28	.005
293	40	20	11	−8	28	.005
394	30	30	15	−8	28	.005
395	30	30	−15	−8	28	.005
396	20	40	−10	−8	28	.005
397	20	40	10	−8	28	.005
398	10	50	10	−8	28	.005
399	10	50	−10	−8	28	.005

Fig.	R	S	T	N	M	Suggested Step Size
400	40	20	10	10	−26	.005
401	40	20	−10	10	−26	.005
402	30	30	−11	10	−26	.005
403	30	30	11	10	−26	.005
404	20	40	11	10	−26	.005
405	20	40	−11	10	−26	.005
406	40	20	12	7/2	−13/2	.025
407	40	20	−12	7/2	−13/2	.025
408	30	30	−15	7/2	−13/2	.025
409	30	30	15	7/2	−13/2	.025
410	20	40	13	7/2	−13/2	.025
411	20	40	−13	7/2	−13/2	.015
412	40	20	15	9/2	−19/2	.015
413	40	20	−15	9/2	−19/2	.015
414	30	30	−17	9/2	−19/2	.015
415	30	30	17	9/2	−19/2	.015
416	20	40	15	9/2	−19/2	.015
417	20	40	−15	9/2	−19/2	.015
418	40	20	−11	−3/5	29/5	.05
419	40	20	11	−3/5	29/5	.05
420	50	10	10	13/5	−19/5	.025
421	50	10	−10	13/5	−19/5	.025
422	40	20	−9	13/5	−19/5	.025
423	40	20	9	13/5	−19/5	.025
424	40	20	20	13/5	−19/5	.025
425	40	20	−20	13/5	−19/5	.025
426	30	30	18	13/5	−19/5	.025
427	30	30	−18	13/5	−19/5	.025
428	20	40	19	13/5	−19/5	.025
429	20	40	−19	13/5	−19/5	.025
430	40	20	12	−7/3	11	.015
431	40	20	−12	−7/3	11	.015
432	30	30	−11	−7/3	11	.015
433	30	30	11	−7/3	11	.015
434	20	40	15	−7/3	11	.015

Fig.	R	S	T	N	M	Suggested Step Size
435	20	40	−15	−7/3	11	.015
436	50	10	12	13/3	−9	.015
437	50	10	15	13/3	−9	.015
438	40	20	−13	13/3	−9	.015
439	40	20	13	13/3	−9	.015
440	30	30	17	13/3	−9	.015
441	30	30	−17	13/3	−9	.015
442	20	40	−16	13/3	−9	.015
443	20	40	16	13/3	−9	.015
444	10	50	16	13/3	−9	.015
445	30	30	11	−5	−29	.01
446	30	30	−11	−5	−29	.01
447	20	40	−12	−5	−29	.01
448	20	40	12	−5	−29	.01
449	10	50	15	−5	−29	.01
450	10	50	−15	−5	−29	.01
451	40	20	11	7	31	.005
452	40	20	−11	7	31	.005
453	30	30	−12	7	31	.005
454	30	30	12	7	31	.005
455	20	40	14	7	31	.005
456	20	40	−14	7	31	.005
457	10	50	−16	7	31	.005
458	10	50	16	7	31	.005
459	40	20	10	−8	31	.005
460	40	20	−10	−8	−44	.005
461	30	30	−11	−8	−44	.005
462	30	30	11	−8	−44	.005
463	20	40	12	−8	−44	.005
464	20	40	−12	−8	−44	.005
465	10	50	−17	−8	−44	.005
466	10	50	17	−8	−44	.005
467	40	20	10	10	46	.005
468	40	20	−10	10	46	.005
469	30	30	12	10	46	.005

Fig.	R	S	T	N	M	Suggested Step Size
470	30	30	−12	10	46	.005
471	20	40	−13	10	46	.005
472	20	40	13	10	46	.005
473	10	50	17	10	46	.005
474	10	50	−17	10	46	.005
475	30	30	12	7/2	27/2	.01
476	30	30	−12	7/2	27/2	.01
477	20	40	−12	7/2	27/2	.01
478	20	40	12	7/2	27/2	.01
479	10	50	15	7/2	27/2	.01
480	10	50	−15	7/2	27/2	.01
481	30	30	9	−5/2	−33/2	.015
482	30	30	−9	−5/2	−33/2	.015
483	20	40	−12	−5/2	−33/2	.015
484	20	40	12	−5/2	−33/2	.015
485	10	50	13	−5/2	−33/2	.015
486	10	50	−13	−5/2	−33/2	.015
487	50	10	−7	9/2	37/2	.015
488	50	10	7	9/2	37/2	.015
489	40	20	11	9/2	37/2	.015
490	40	20	−11	9/2	37/2	.015
491	30	30	−13	9/2	37/2	.015
492	30	30	13	9/2	37/2	.015
493	20	40	14	9/2	37/2	.015
494	20	40	−14	9/2	37/2	.015
495	10	50	15	9/2	37/2	.015
496	10	50	−15	9/2	37/2	.015
497	40	20	11	−3/5	−7	.035
498	40	20	−11	−3/5	−7	.035
499	30	30	−10	−3/5	−7	.035
500	30	30	10	−3/5	−7	.035
501	10	50	−12	−3/5	−7	.035
502	10	50	12	−3/5	−7	.035
503	50	10	9	13/5	9	.025
504	50	10	−9	13/5	9	.025

Fig.	R	S	T	N	M	Suggested Step Size
505	40	20	−9	13/5	9	.025
506	40	20	9	13/5	9	.025
507	30	30	11	13/5	9	.025
508	30	30	−11	13/5	9	.025
509	20	40	−12	13/5	9	.025
510	20	40	12	13/5	9	.025
511	40	20	−11	−7/3	−47/3	.015
512	40	20	11	−7/3	−47/3	.015
513	30	30	12	−7/3	−47/3	.015
514	30	30	−12	−7/3	−47/3	.015
515	20	40	−11	−7/3	−47/3	.015
516	20	40	11	−7/3	−47/3	.015
517	10	50	13	−7/3	−47/3	.015
518	10	50	−13	−7/3	−47/3	.015
519	50	10	−8	13/3	53/3	.015
520	50	10	8	13/3	53/3	.015
521	40	20	13	13/3	53/3	.01
522	40	20	−13	13/3	53/3	.01
523	30	30	−13	13/3	53/3	.01
524	30	30	13	13/3	53/3	.01
525	20	40	17	13/3	53/3	.01
526	20	40	−17	13/3	53/3	.01
527	10	50	−18	13/3	53/3	.01
528	10	50	18	13/3	53/3	.01
529	10	50	10	7	−29	.005
530	30	30	4	−8	46	.005
531	30	30	−5	−8	46	.005
532	20	40	−2	−8	46	.005
533	20	40	6	−8	46	.005
534	30	30	−5	10	−44	.005
535	30	30	−9	7/2	−23/2	.015
536	30	30	9	7/2	−23/2	.015
537	20	40	10	7/2	−23/2	.015
538	20	40	−10	7/2	−23/2	.015
539	20	40	−5	−5/2	37/2	.015

Fig.	R	S	T	N	M	Suggested Step Size
540	40	20	−4	9/2	−33/2	.015
541	30	30	3	9/2	−33/2	.015
542	30	30	−4	13/5	−7	.025
543	20	40	5	13/5	−7	.025
544	10	50	5	−7/3	53/3	.015
545	30	30	5	13/3	−47/3	.015
546	20	40	9	13/3	−47/3	.015
547	30	30	−5	10	64	.0025
548	20	40	−10	10	64	.0025
549	20	40	10	10	64	.0025
550	40	20	4	−3/5	−51/5	.025
551	30	30	−8	−3/5	−51/5	.025
552	30	30	8	−3/5	−51/5	.025
553	40	20	−7	13/5	61/5	.025
554	40	20	7	13/5	61/5	.025
555	30	30	10	13/5	61/5	.025
556	30	30	−10	13/5	61/5	.025
557	20	40	−10	13/5	61/5	.025
558	20	40	10	13/5	61/5	.025
559	30	30	9	−7/3	−67/3	.025
560	30	30	−9	−7/3	−67/3	.025
561	20	40	−3	−7/3	−67/3	.025
562	40	20	9	13/3	73/3	.01
563	40	20	−9	13/3	73/3	.01
564	30	30	−10	13/3	73/3	.01
565	40	20	5	9/2	−27	.015
566	40	20	−5	9/2	−27	.015
567	30	30	−3	9/2	−27	.015
568	40	20	6	13/5	−59/5	.025
569	40	20	−6	13/5	−59/5	.025
570	30	30	−4	13/5	−59/5	0.25
571	30	30	4	13/5	−59/5	.025
572	20	40	−5	13/5	−59/5	.025
573	20	40	−3	−7/3	83/3	.015
574	30	30	5	13/3	−77/3	.015

Fig.	R	S	T	N	M	Suggested Step Size
575	30	30	3	10	91	.005
576	30	30	7	−3/5	−15	.015
577	30	30	14	−8	29/2	.01
578	20	40	17	−8	29/2	.01
579	50	10	10	10	−25/2	.01
580	30	30	15	10	−25/2	.01
581	20	40	20	10	−25/2	.01
582	50	10	20	7/2	−11/4	.05
583	20	40	13	−5/2	25/4	.025
584	10	50	16	−5/2	25/4	.025
585	20	40	17	7	−14	.01
586	40	20	5	10	−20	.01
587	40	20	10	10	−20	.01
588	50	5	5	55	−53	.005
589	45	20	15	57	−53	.005
590	47	15	14	55	−50	.005
591	50	15	18	55	−49	.005
592	50	10	8	61	−50	.005
593	36	28	24	56	−55	.001
594	45	30	12	−54	110	.001
595	44	24	21.6	57/2	−27	.001
596	44	24	21.6	−54	57	.001
597	44	24	21.6	−53/2	29	.001